CW00499127

SEMIOTEXT(E) FOREIGN AGENTS SERIES

Originally published as *Quando il verbo si fa carne. Linguaggio e natura umana.*
© 2003 Paolo Virno and Bollati Boringhieri, editore, Torino.
© This edition 2015 by Semiotext(e)

All rights reserved. No part of this book may be reproduced, stored in a retrieval system, or transmitted by any means, electronic, mechanical, photocopying, recording, or otherwise, without prior permission of the publisher.

Published by Semiotext(e)
PO BOX 629, South Pasadena, CA 91031
www.semiotexte.com

Special thanks to John Ebert.

Cover art: Christopher Williams, *Bouquet, for Bas Jan Ader and Christopher D'Arcangelo*, 1991. Archival corrugated board, archival photocorners, compound, 4-ply Conservamat, 8-ply Conservamat, drywall, dye transfer print, glass, lacquer-based finish, linen tape, nails, Northern maple, plastic setback strips, primer, screws, seaming tape, paint, and wood. Print: 16 x 20 inches. Wall: 120 x 180 x 4 3/4 inches. Courtesy David Zwirner, New York/London and Galerie Gisela Capitain, Cologne.

Design by Hedi El Kholti

ISBN: 978-1-58435-094-1
Distributed by The MIT Press, Cambridge, Mass. and London, England
Printed in the United States of America

WHEN THE WORD BECOMES FLESH

LANGUAGE AND HUMAN NATURE

Paolo Virno

Translated by Giuseppina Mecchia

<e>

Contents

Giuseppina Mecchia

Preface

Readers familiar with Paolo Virno's political philosophy might be surprised to read a book as deeply steeped in early and mid-20th century linguistics, philosophy of language and phenomenology as *When The Word Becomes Flesh*. It is of course true that, originally published in Italian in 2002, roughly at the same time as *A Grammar of the Multitude*—a series of lectures presented by Virno at the University of Calabria and translated into English by Semiotext(e) in 2004—this book is to a certain extent a more detailed philosophical presentation of the same theses. And indeed, some arguments recur quite literally: the radical questioning of the private dimension of mental life, the analogy between the speaker and the musical virtuoso, the attention given to theories of individuation, and the rethinking of the Marxian category of "general intellect" in the context of contemporary forms of labor. In this respect, the book could almost be considered a more philosophically complex companion to the previous one.

And yet this is a rather different book, which reconfigures Virno's positions on a rather different conceptual terrain. *A Grammar of the Multitude* declared its political intent from the very beginning, with an Introduction that found its point of departure in the definition of people and multitude in Hobbes and Spinoza, and continued with a discussion of Marx's definition of general intellect. The centrality of the linguistic faculty to political action was of course already there, not only in the title, but also in the references to Aristotle and Saussure contained in the book's second chapter. However, if on the one hand *When the Word Becomes Flesh* picks up where *A Grammar of the Multitude* lets off—notably the issue of bio-politics and of the affective nature of language exchanges and political involvement—on the other it also develops a much expanded, more detailed and maybe slightly different foundation to Virno's reflection on the politics of language.

1. From post-workerism to a phenomenology of the political subject

In his introduction to the English edition of *A Grammar of the Multitude*, Sylvère Lotringer gave an excellent account of Virno's intellectual and political trajectory within the Italian movement now widely known as *Operaismo* (workerism).[1] In the last decade, this term has become much more familiar to the general readership, and the theses of the thinkers involved in that movement have been aired in many different venues: we are in a new stage of capital development, where value is extracted not only from structured labor, but from the entire potential of the human subject. In the age of information and entertainment, language itself, as a faculty, is now monetized and sold for a profit. The "multitude" is the human subject as thinking and speaking animal, whose available potential for creation and expression perfectly coincides with its potential for exploitation. As Lotringer said, recognizing that the multitude is the subject of language and therefore of value creation is not a guarantee of political relevance and even less of social justice: since the multitude is a diffused general intellect and not a class, "it can't build a class consciousness of its own, let alone engage capital in a class struggle."[2] There is no easy political project to be followed once the full potential of the human animal is analyzed and brought to light. Still, reflecting on what we are and what we can be as talking and thinking beings helps us to keep in mind that the subject of capital is indeed the same as the subject of communism: the human animal as form of life and worldly relation. This is why in *When the Word Becomes Flesh*, Virno strays quite far from Marxism and political philosophy, adopting what may best be defined as a post-phenomenological point of view.

The shift in argumentation might be best introduced through a brief analysis of the title and its distinctively biblical resonance. The centrality of the linguistic function to political action was previously underscored through the mentioning of a "grammar" of political subjectivity, here language first appears as "Word," which traditionally denotes the word of God. In the Christian tradition, there are at least two distinctive events which witness the transformation of such a word into "flesh": the first one is of course the act of creation, and the second is the incarnation of Jesus Christ as god-man. One important philosophical aspect of both these incarnations is the temporal one: creation inaugurates cosmic time, while the advent of Christ and of salvation gives to human time a new eschatological dimension, guaranteeing a return to the eternity of the Word after experiencing the transience of the flesh.

And indeed, an analysis of the title's conceptual foundations introduces a striking aspect of the philosophical method adopted by Virno in this book: the secularization of concepts and expressions tied to religious language, with the aim of accounting for two fundamentally different aspects of human temporality and historicity. The Christian reconciliation of God's eternal thought and his transient, immanent creation, the dual nature of Jesus Christ, the simultaneous absence and presence of God in the experience of the praying subject: these are the analogic bases for introducing the secular distinctions that are at the core of Virno's argument in *When the Word Becomes Flesh*. They are also based on the difficult relation between "invariable" and "variable" characteristics, although in the secular realm we no longer deal with eternity and human time, but with invariable human nature and variable historical contexts.

The linguistic faculty is for Virno the defining invariable attribute of the human animal, as it has stabilized with the advent of *Homo sapiens* during the Cro Magnon age. This faculty guarantees a continuity in the potentialities offered to all human beings at the moment of their birth, and remains an insuppressible dynamic force available in the most different socio-historical conditions. In this respect, he fully agrees with the position of Noam Chomsky described in chapter 6, although Chomsky speaks more broadly of "human intelligence." Virno, however, parts ways with the American linguist when the latter thinks that a defense of the natural patrimony of the human animal could constitute a political program as such. The main problem, for Virno, is that Chomsky considers that each human being has access, as individual, to the entirety of the linguistic faculty, and is therefore always able to realize his or her own potentialities unless explicitly prevented from doing so by a totalitarian imposition of force.

This is when Virno's recourse to the contributions of Lev Vygotsky and Gilbert Simondon proves absolutely decisive: since the linguistic faculty lies dormant waiting for its actualization in a public space, Virno considers language a transindividual reality, which always presupposes a public exchange. The human species, precisely because it is capable of speech, is not composed by separate individuals, but rather remains both the theater and the audience for any linguistic performance. In chapter 7, Virno underscores the importance of Vygotksy's insight that the human being proceeds "from the social to the individual," and not the other way around.

Even more decisive, for Virno's theses, is the fact, stressed by Simondon, that the pre-individual, species-related characters of every individuated being are still at work in constituting it as a subject. In other words, when I become a subject of speech, I speak not only as an individuated being, but also as a social being belonging to a transindividual reality. Unless I fully engage with this pre- and trans-individual human characterization, I cannot even develop any individual traits: in this respect, the linguistic faculty and our mental and affective abilities are inseparable, since without language I could not, in any way, become a subject.

But once I am a subject of speech, I do belong to a trans-individual, fully historical—incarnated, so to speak—domain, which guarantees by political agency since my speech makes me appear on the public sphere, at once distinct from and fully embedded within a multitude of linguistic subjects all connected to each other by speech itself.

There is, however, an important *caveat* to this rather hopeful understanding of the politics of language: the linguistic faculty does not guarantee any particular political action, it is neither the purveyor nor the guarantor of justice, equality or freedom. What it does, is to redefine the Marxist notion of "social individual" on a phenomenological basis, defining what Virno calls "the many as many" as political subject.

2. From mysticism to natural history

One might object to Virno that his definition of social bonds still depends solely on a-historical notions: the species, the individuated being, and the transindividual subject of speech. We remain in the phenomenological realm even with Virno's notion of "natural history," since the history that is described is the same for every individuated member of the species. This is why the many as many have *no particular politics*, but only a *political nature*. Can this be a sufficient foundation for a truly political philosophy? To a certain extent, Virno builds concepts that mark a void, an empty space incapable of thinking its own future realizations. There is a mystical undertone to this absence, one that Virno fully acknowledges, and nowhere more so in his Appendix on Wittgenstein, which provides a most significant closing to this remarkably complex work.

Wittgenstein had made his appearance in the very first chapter of the book, providing Virno with some important steps in his argument: first and foremost, the later works of the Austrian philosopher had provided a definition of language as an activity that does not depend on external definitions or goals in order to develop: a language game creates its own rules, independently from the truth contained in its statements. In this respect, the Wittgenstein of the *Logical Investigations* and the *Philosophical Grammar* is a valuable ally in Virno's attempt at defining an immanent, if invariable, linguistic faculty.

In the Appendix, however, Virno goes back to Wittgenstein's first—and only—published work, the *Tractatus Logico-Philosophicus*, which provides a rigorous attempt at systematizing and transcribing in logical terms possible true statements and their relation with the facts of the world. Without going into excessively technical detail, we can say that this one aspect of the *Tractatus* situates Wittgenstein quite close to his masters, Frege and Russell, and their American disciple, Noam Chomsky. But of course, the *Tractatus* does not stop there, since Wittgenstein immediately debunks his own work by proclaiming its profound vacuity. All these "logical propositions" that present "the scaffolding of the world," still tell us nothing about what we want to know. As Virno rightly points out, the early Wittgenstein does not content himself with language and logic and their spatio-temporal fields of application, since what is wanted is nothing less than "the riddle of life," whose sense is situated outside language, and therefore is logically non-sensical. Thence the famous appeal at the end of the *Tractatus*, that has been widely interpreted as a condemnation not only of metaphysics, but of philosophy tout court: "Whereof one cannot speak, thereof one must be silent."

There is little doubt that, as Virno says, this is a mystical attitude on the part of Wittgenstein, which risks emptying out all meaning for the linguistic exchange, since in any case it cannot say anything about what matters most. What is more important, though, is that in the Appendix Virno points out that even the later Wittgenstein doesn't really overcome this mystical stance, contrary to what is commonly said about his philosophical development. This is why, after having used Wittgenstein's later works in order to build his own conceptual apparatus, Virno distances himself from him in the Appendix.

Wittgenstein's critique of philosophy stems from a deeply religious standpoint: human language perfectly coincides with the human world, and therefore cannot address its own—and the world's—meaning. For Virno, on the contrary, what is needed is an *atheist* critique of philosophy: we should replace our conceptual referents in such a way that the human being would not be seen as shut off from the meaning of a world, but as fully immersed in an environment—an *Umwelt*—subject to all the vicissitudes of what he calls a *natural history*. Language, as natural faculty, is part and parcel of the human environment, and therefore does not simply have the task of describe an external object—the world as defined by Wittgenstein—but is fully embedded in its material-sensorial environment. We can perceive our world, although we might not be able to fully know it. And language can always be articulated, although never fully realized.

We understand, now, what are the stakes of Virno's critique of Wittgenstein: if the linguistic faculty, ultimately, is what insures that the political potentials of the human being can never be suppressed, we need to be able to bring it fully into the domain of immanence and historical change. This is why the only counter-discourse with respect to metaphysical, atemporal definitions of the human being have to be founded in what he calls "a natural history," that is, the vicissitudes of the human animal in human time.

This is a tall order indeed. But we should not be afraid to follow Virno in his perilous path of conceptual exploration, since what is at stake might very well be our belief that a political agency is always conceivable even in the darkest turns of our collective "natural history."

— Giuseppina Mecchia, University of Pittsburgh

Introduction

This book contains several philosophical reflections on language, that is, on human nature. Although each chapter has an independent beginning, these reflections are systematic, and have to be read in the order of their presentation. Almost all arguments are the premise or the consequence of the others. Jumping around the chapters will lead to serious misunderstandings.

The book spirals around its object tracing ever larger concentric circles.

The first part (ch. 1–3) is devoted to the macrocosm of enunciation. To speak: this familiar and unpretentious event constitutes nonetheless the most credible experimental basis for addressing some of the most important philosophical issues. The analysis of the different components of a verbal elocution allows us to come to a few, nonobvious conclusions about the distinctive traits of human praxis: the relation between power and action, the formation of self-awareness, the principle of individuation, and the origins of the religious instance. Each enunciation, in short, resumes on a Lilliputian scale the most salient steps of anthropogenesis.

The second part (ch. 4–5) deals with the biblical "incarnation of the Word." The discussion addresses the sensible, external and perceptible reality of words. This explains the attempt to redefine and rehabilitate two notions that, in their current definitions, have a terrible reputation: physiognomy and reification. These chapters would like to reveal the essentially *public* character of the linguistic mind.

The third part (ch. 6–7) widens immensely our perspective. Here we examine the relation between biological invariants and changing historical experiences. The earlier considerations on the structure of the enunciation and the public nature of the mind find their macroscopic correspondences in the concept (also redefined with respect to its habitual meaning) of *natural history*. This concept can greatly help in the description of contemporary forms of life and the sketching of political categories adequate to the understanding of a mode of production that finds language at its very core.

In many chapters we mention in passing the logical-linguistic issue of atheism. We have said logical-linguistic, not psychological or moral. The Appendix tries to flesh out these remarks, with an analysis of the religious critique addressed by Wittgenstein to traditional philosophy.

I would like to define the idea constituting the recurring *refrain* of all chapters in the book in the simplest of ways. There is always time for complicating things.

There are, doubtlessly, some very general preconditions for our experience as human animals: language, self-awareness, historicity and so forth. In Kantian terms we would call them transcendental conditions; in Heideggerian terms, ontological foundations. In evolutionist terms, finally, we would speak of species-specific prerogatives. Now, it is widely believed that these fundamental conditions, that determine the facts and state of affairs punctuating our lives, never appear as facts or state of affairs. They would seem to cause all sorts of contingent phenomena, but without disposing of their own phenomenal evidence. But this book strenuously opposes this conviction.

It is my intention to show that the conditions making experience possible are themselves the object of an immediate experience, that transcendental presuppositions manifest themselves as such in several common empirical occurrences, and that ontological foundations are humbly placed within the world of appearances. The book takes stock of the different occasions when the background comes to the fore, assuming the role of fact among facts. In other words, there are occasions when human nature knows its own full *revelation*. Exempt from all theological flirtation, this term refers simply to the entirely empirical visibility of what we wrongly believed inaccessible to direct perception. The titles of the different chapters designate the categories most apt to think this wholly materialistic "revelation": the absolute performative, the anthropogenetic repetition, a second-degree sensorialism, reification, and natural history.

A stenographic anticipation of the book's theses would be futile. A preliminary summary is always too little or too much and has the confounding ability to obscure that which by itself is not subject to doubt. It will suffice to say that these theses will irk both the disciples of hermeneutics and the high priests of cognitive science. The first will protest against their unbridled naturalism; the second, their willingness to seriously consider many essentially metaphysical questions. I would like to believe that both contestations are justified. In fact, taken together, I consider them involuntary praises. Those who really want to deal with "the animal possessing language," have to consider as fully *natural* even the antinomies of pure reason.

I have had the privilege to discuss at length the themes of the book with Daniele Gambarara. I owe much to my engagement with Stefano Catucci, Felice Cimatti, Massimo De Carolis, Augusto Illuminati, Marco Mazzeo. Some parts of the text have benefited—to an extent that I can't fully gauge—from a propitious rereading of Emilio Garroni's *Senso e Paradosso* (1986).[1] It has also been good, for myself and for my book, to have recently stumbled into Franco Lo Piparo's linguistic-philosophical essays.

The first drafts of one or more chapters have been read and commented by Francesca Borrelli, Francesco Ferretti, Sara Fortuna, Giovanni Garroni, Michael Hardt, Ivan Maffezzani, Christian Marazzi, Sandro Piperno, Francesco Raparelli, Tommaso Russo, Livia Schiller, Alberto Toscano e Benedetto Vecchi. I am grateful to all of them. I also want to thank Paolo Leonardi for his corrosive critique of chapter 2.

These reflections on language and human nature see as their horizon the first political movement that explicitly addressed the essential prerogatives of our species. I am talking about the men and women who filled the streets of Genoa in 2001,[2] rescuing the public sphere from the atrocious caricatures that so often deface it.

Part 1

The Act of Speaking

Our subject is the act of enunciating itself, not the text of the enunciation.

— Emile Benveniste

Even before meaning something, each linguistic emission signals that someone is speaking. This decisive fact has been neglected by linguists. Before acting as the vector of specific messages, the voice already says a whole lot.

— Paul Valéry

Speak, so that I may see you.

— Georg C. Lichtenberg

1

The Speaker as Performing Artist

1. Saussure's symphony

At the very beginning of his *Course in General Linguistics*, Saussure suggests almost casually an analogy laden with implications: "Language is comparable to a symphony in that what the symphony actually is stands completely apart from how it is performed."[1] The similitude, formulated with didactic intents (so much so that a completely different one can be found soon after: language as dictionary), wants to underscore the autonomy of a *language system* with respect to the accidental variations punctuating concrete utterances. However, if we take the comparison seriously, that is to say literally, it allows us to establish a solid link between structural linguistics and the philosophy of praxis, a nexus between Saussure's *Course* and Aristotle's *Nicomachean Ethics*.

What really matters here is the less visible aspect of Saussure's parallel: if language functions like a musical score, the experience of the speaker can be reasonably compared to that of the performing artist. Whoever starts to speak would therefore behave just like a pianist, a dancer or an actor. Speaking would then mean showing off those qualities that, pushed to their limits, are usually considered the prerogative of virtuoso performers. But is it really so? Before testing (or eventually radicalizing) this hypothesis, it is useful to clarify what is at stake here.

2. Activities without work

What characterizes the work of the performing artist? Mostly two things: first of all, these actions have no extrinsic goal. They don't create a lasting product, since they only aim at their own occurrence. They don't create new objects, but rather a contingent and singular event ("and then Sarah Bernhardt imparted an ironic nuance to the final monologue," or "in Montreal, Glenn Gould suddenly toned down the *andante con brio*"). At the end of the play, or of the concert, nothing remains. The pianist or the actor performs an *activity without Work*. Or, if you prefer, the purpose of their activity coincides entirely with its own execution. Secondly, musicians and actors need the presence of others: their ephemeral *performance* only exists if it is seen or heard, and therefore only when there is a "public." These two characteristics are deeply linked: the virtuoso needs a public precisely because he is not leaving behind any object that would remain in the world once the performance is over. An activity without work always implies, for structural reasons, the subject's exposure to the gaze, and sometimes the harsh reaction, of his fellow humans.

The work of the performing artist can be easily included in the conceptual constellation of book VI in the *Nicomachean Ethics*. Aristotle opposes the production of previously non-existing things to real action, and also—but basically it is the same thing—work to politics. Production (*poiesis*) enabled by a technique has an exterior goal, since it finds its realization in an independent object. "And every art is concerned with bringing something into being, i.e., with contriving or calculating how to bring into being some one of those things that can either be or not be."[2] Ethical-political action (*praxis*), which is sustained by the capacity to decide what it takes "to live well in an absolute sense" (*eu zen olos*) finds instead its realization in itself and is therefore similar to the performances of the musician or the dancer.

> Prudence cannot be either a science or an art: it cannot be a science because the sphere of action is that which is alterable; it cannot be an action, because production is generically different from action. It follows from all this that prudence is a formed faculty that apprehends truth by reasoning or calculation, and issues in action, in the domain of human good and ill; for while production has another end than itself, this is not so with action, since good action or well doing is itself its end.[3]

The way a cellist or a dancer operates is neither strange nor marginal. It is, on the very contrary, the iconic recapitulation of all the characteristics that define human *praxis* in general. Contingency, instability, absence of purpose, inseparability between the "product" and the actions that realize it, necessary institution of a public sphere: all of these define ethical and political conduct (and before that, game playing). It was Hannah Arendt, the most daring Aristotelian of the 20th century, who noticed this similarity when she said that "the performing arts, on the contrary, have indeed a strong affinity with politics. Performing artists—dancers, play-actors, musicians, and the like—need an audience to show their virtuosity, just as acting men need the presence of others before whom they can appear."[4]

3. The verbal virtuoso

But let's go back to Saussure's metaphor. If language is a symphony, the speaker shares the same characteristics as the performing artist. Being contingent and singular, each *speech act* boils down to a virtuoso performance. It does not create an independent object and therefore it implies the presence of others. This means that linguistic activity, considered as a whole, is neither production (*poiesis*) nor cognition (*episteme*), but action (*praxis*).

Human language has not Work to realize, because it is not a tool to be employed in order to realize external goals. Emile Benveniste wrote the following:

> In fact, the comparison of language to an instrument—and it should necessarily be a material instrument for the comparison even to be comprehensible—must fill us with mistrust, as should every simplistic notion about language. To speak of an instrument is to put man and nature in opposition. The pick, the arrow, and the wheel are not in nature. They are fabrications. Language is the nature of man, and he did not fabricate it. We are always inclined to that naïve concept of a primordial period in which a complete man discovered another one, equally complete, and between the two of them language was worked out little by little. This is a pure fiction. We can never get back to man separated from language and we shall never see him inventing it.[5]

The speaker performs a self-fulfilling action, just like seeing or breathing. Speaking, seeing and breathing are actions that manifest the way of being of a particular biological organism and cooperate toward its "living well in an absolute sense." We don't speak because we have observed that the use of language is advantageous to us: we speak as we live, but not because we consider life useful.

However, it is undeniable that we use language to attain innumerable specific goals: to intimidate, to seduce, to move, to deceive, to measure an area, to unleash an air bombing, organize a labor strike and so on. Innumerable, therefore, are the occasions when language seems a tool that we can use to achieve non-linguistic goals. We should notice, though, that the goals achieved *through* language, are only conceivable, as such, *on the basis* of language: this is why they are nonetheless the goals *of* language. To paraphrase Wittgenstein, "I know what I long for before I get it" precisely and only because "I have learned to talk." Or else, categorically: "It is in language that an expectation and its fulfillment make contact."[6]

And yet this is not the most important point. Let's admit for a moment that many of our enunciations have extra-linguistic goals. The fact remains, far more decisive, that we can't explain the enunciating activity and its peculiar laws by either one of these extrinsic ends or a consideration of them as a whole. Believing this would be akin to pretending to explain the rules of a game through the different effects that it can have on the players (amusement, boredom, the cultivation of friendships or rivalries). This pretense, however, is perfectly legitimate when we are dealing not with a virtuoso *praxis*, but with a *poiesis* aimed at building an autonomous product: it is the house—that is, the end result—that determines the smallest details and procedures of the building process.

Verbal praxis is not dependent on extra-linguistic goals, just as a memorable piano *performance* is not dependent on the pianist's desire for riches. A counter-proof for this argument is that the pertinence or the *perfection* (in the sense of the "perfection" of a dancer's pirouette or a singer's pitch) of our sentences can't be measured on the basis of their consequences. As Wittgenstein writes:

> If I want to carve a block of wood into a particular shape, any cut that gives it the right shape is a good one. But I don't call an argument a good argument just because it has the consequences that I want (Pragmatism). I may call a calculation wrong even if the action based on its result has led to the desired end.[7]

The polemic allusion to pragmatism deserves our attention. It would be wrong to believe that Wittgenstein criticizes the pragmatists for having neglected the cognitive value of enunciations. Nothing is further from the truth. As paradoxical as it might seem, their real limitation was that they did not recognize that language is *praxis*, and that it constitutes, therefore, its own end and norm. By judging pertinent the enunciations achieving certain extra-linguistic goals, pragmatism ruinously assimilates the speaker's activity to *poiesis*.

4. Cooking and speaking

The distinction between acting (*pratteing*) and producing (*poiesis*), which dominates the book 4 of the *Nicomachean Ethics*, is referenced by Wittgenstein almost literally in his *Philosophical Grammar*. Except that here, acting is identified with language. In a long series of related passages, Wittgenstein shows us the logical distinction that separates the rules of linguistic practice and those regulating the fabrication of an artifact. The first are *arbitrary*, while the second are not, since they are dictated by the specific properties of the artifact constituting the end of the productive process:

> Why don't I call cookery rules arbitrary, and why am I tempted to call the rules of grammar arbitrary? Because I think of the concept "cookery" as defined by the end of cookery, and I don't think of the concept "language" as defined by the end of language. You cook badly if you are guided in your cooking by rules other than the right ones; but if you follow other rules than those of chess you are playing another game; and if you follow grammatical rules other than such and such ones, that does not mean that you say something wrong, no, you are speaking of something else.[8]

Since it is not defined by any occasional purpose, language stipulates its own rules. "The rules of grammar may be called 'arbitrary,' if that is to mean that the aim of the grammar is nothing but that of language."[9] The measuring unit cannot be separated from what needs to be measured: on the contrary, it *institutes* the phenomenon to which it applies. In other words, the rule does not limit itself to the administration of the relation between meanings and reality, but it presides over the creation of every meaning. "There cannot be a question whether these or other rules are the correct ones for the use of 'not' (that is, whether they accord with its meaning). For without these rules the word has as yet no meaning; and if we change the rules, it now has another meaning (or none), and in that case we may just as well change the word too."[10] Besides establishing a clear distinction between language and production, the arbitrariness of rules also dispels the cognitivist illusion according to which the task of human elocution would be to communicate already thought thoughts. On the one end, as it was shown by the example of the "not," there are many thoughts that language alone makes possible. On the other, and always by virtue of the same arbitrariness, there are many enunciations that carry no epistemic value whatsoever:

which thought would be expressed by "damn it," "help me" or "Oh my God"? Let's repeat it once more: neither *poiesis* nor *episteme*, human language is first and foremost *praxis*.

"Arbitrary" means "natural": the two terms imply each other, and are sometimes synonymous. If language were an artifact, that is, a tool, it would be subject to invariable rules derived from the best way to use it. But as Benveniste said, language is in the nature of man, who did not create it. Verbal praxis is a trait characteristic of our species. Differently from animal communication, whose every single sign univocally corresponds to a particular environmental occurrence (a specific danger, the possibility of finding food, and so on), human speech can be broken up into "elements of articulation, devoid of meaning. It is the selective and distinctive grouping of these elements of articulation which produces the sense units"[11] Language, therefore, is a biological activity independent from environmental considerations. It is an end in itself, and its results perfectly coincide with its execution. This kind of self-fulfilling activity can only be self-regulated. The arbitrariness of linguistic rules is therefore natural, and even necessary. "The only correlate in language to an intrinsic necessity is an arbitrary rule. It is the only thing which one can milk out of this intrinsic necessity into a preposition."[12]

Wittgenstein thinks that life and language are co-extensive concepts:

> 'It is always for living beings that signs exist, so that must be something essential to a sign.' Yes, but how is a 'living' being defined? It appears that here I am prepared to use its capacity to use a sign-language as a defining mark of a living being. And the concept of a living being really has an indeterminacy very similar to that of the concept 'language.'[13]

Life and language share the same indeterminacy because, being deprived of any extrinsic purpose, they both obey arbitrary rules. But it is this same indeterminacy that opens up the space for an object whose value is precisely "that which is alterable." Our enunciations delineate a kind of *naturalistic virtuosity*. If this is the case, we need to radicalize our initial comparison. The model for all other activity without a product is language, as the matrix of any virtuoso performance. The performing artist is simply restaging, in highly specialized forms, the experience of the speaker.

5. Language as transitional phenomenon

Historiographical commonplaces are unfair, but as it happens with unfounded suspicions, they are often right, in that they reveal something important. People often say that Chomsky's rebuttal of Skinner's theses in his review of *Verbal Behavior* inaugurated a new era in the philosophy of the mind. People say that while behaviorism considered language a public tool that is appropriated by the individual thanks to the conditioning influence of his social environment, Chomsky and cognitive science reestablished his character of biological attribute naturally shared by each member of the species. We say that we have gone from a language-tool, extrinsically determined, to a language-organ, independent from historical context and entirely situated *in interiore hominis*. This is just a historiographical commonplace. There is no need to discuss its accuracy, or to complicate its theses. The Chomsky-Skinner dispute is educational precisely because of its schematic, parable-like organization. What the parable demonstrates is how difficult it is to understand language as *the biological organ for public praxis*. The oscillation between pragmatist sociability (like in the inferior "pragmatism" attacked by Wittgenstein) and depoliticized mentalism—or in more specialized words, between *poiesis* and *episteme*—seems utterly inevitable.

If we want to stop this oscillation and mitigate the difficulties of this dilemma, we need to restack the cards and start a new game. Linguistic praxis escapes the alternative between "interior" and "exterior," between inscrutable mental representation and solid objective reality. Rather, it configures the preliminary *intermediate zone* whence both polarities originate. In the beginning (in a logical sense of course) there is the Word as Action. Locution rests at the border between I and non-I: it makes possible the distinction between the two realms but it does not belong completely to either one of them. Let's just think about our voice: it is released into the environment as part of our body, but then comes back to the body as part of the environment. Verbal action is both apparent and intimate; exposed to the other's eyes, it is nonetheless inseparable from the contingent person of its performer. Linguistic practice rests in the hiatus between the mind and the world, a gap that cannot be filled by a predetermined conduct but needs to be mastered with virtuoso performances and arbitrary rules. The British psychoanalyst Donald W. Winnicott refers to this hiatus as of a "potential space" where amphibious characters—that is, the mingling of the subjective and the objective—still prevail.[14] And in fact, the human animal is a being that acts precisely because it is not bound to a predetermined vital sphere, and mostly inhabits this indefinite zone. The potential space between mind and world—a true no man's (and every man's) land—is constitutively a *public* space. Except for the fact that this original publicity bears no resemblance to an exterior state of things, nor does it oppose a secret interior reality: if anything, it constitutes the common precondition for the two antipodal terms. Only when this no man's land is colonized by language does a sharp separation between I and non-I emerge, between "inside" and "outside," cognition and behavior.

Verbal action shares many of the characters attributed by Winnicott to the so-called *transitional phenomena*. These are experiences located between the psyche's meanderings (desires, impulses, intentions and so on) and the realm of things and intersubjectively verified facts.

> After the baby is born this substance that joins and also separates becomes represented by objects and phenomena of which it can be said once again that while they are part of the infant they are also part of the environment. Only gradually do we demand of the developing individual that there shall be a fully acknowledged distinction between external reality and inner psychic reality; indeed there is a relic of the intermediate substance in the cultural life of grown men and women, in fact in that which most clearly distinguishes human being from the animals (religion, art, philosophy).[15]

Among the transitional phenomena mentioned by Winnicott, play stands out for its relevance. Just like linguistic praxis and virtuoso performance, play is public but not external (since it does not create a self-standing work "repudiated as a not-me phenomenon"[16]), personal but not internal (since it does not presuppose a mental representation but on the contrary it creates them as its own reverberation or collateral effect). According to Winnicott, while external reality and instinctual legacy present an unquestionable fixity, play is characterized instead by a high degree of variability and contingency. We could say that play illustrates very well the indeterminacy that, in Wittgenstein's eyes, characterizes life and language alike. Last but not least, in transitional phenomena the canonical alternative between innate and acquired faculties loses all relevance, since they are governed by a paradoxical principle: "The child creates an object, but this object would not have been created as such if it had not already been there."[17] Something that already existed on its own is nonetheless reinvented *ex novo*. This is true for play, but also, in all evidence, for verbal activity. Language, as the biological organ for public praxis, is the most important and widespread transitional phenomenon.

6. Without a script

The pianist plays a waltz by Chopin, the actor recites the famous replies of Shakespeare's Julius Caesar, the dancer sticks to a choreography and leaves little to chance. Performing artists, in other words, follow a well-defined script. They don't create a self-standing work, but they still depend on one (the waltz, the play, and so on). Things are different for the speaker: he cannot rely on a specific script. Everything considered, Saussure's comparison is only appropriate in its implicit part, the one that sees the speaker as a musician, but not in its explicit one, that compares language to a symphony. While a symphony is a work articulated in its every detail, an action accomplished in the past (by Beethoven, let's say), the language taken up by the speaker's virtuoso performance constitutes a simple potentiality, without preordained measures nor autonomous parts, since language is, as Saussure himself taught us, a "plexus of eternally negative differences," where every fragment is defined only by its "non-coincidence with the rest."[18] Not only the speaker does not create a work that would differ from his performance, but neither can he anchor his own praxis in a pre-existing work to be revived by the performance. The absence of a self-standing work is visible both at the end and at the beginning of the enunciation-performance. Therefore, the virtuoso nature of the speaker is double: besides not leaving any trace, he doesn't even have a previous trace that he could refer to. This is why the speaker is the most radical and paradigmatic type of performing artist. Linguistic praxis, twice object-less, has as its sole script the amorphous potentiality for speech, the pure and simple ability to talk, the signifying voice. If the excellence of the actor consists in the most appropriate and striking passage from the act-script to the act-performance, the excellence of the speaker is deduced from the way he or she is able to articulate, each time anew, the relation between potentiality and action. And it is this same relation, in fact, that characterizes what we called "natural virtuoso performance," which consists in modulating through self-standing executions the potential *indeterminacy* of life and language.

The fact that the pattern followed by the speaker is a mere potentiality (a *dynamis*), and not a detailed and univocal script, distances the speaker's activity from other performances, but it also brings it closer to the Aristotelian notion of praxis. While the latter is discussed in Book VI of the *Nicomachean Ethics*, the sharp distinction between ethical-political praxis and work is founded in two different modalities of the relation potentiality-action examined in Book IX of *Metaphysics*. Aristotle distinguishes between acts that simply exhibit their corresponding potentiality and always return to it in a circular manner, and those that move away from it according to a unidirectional progression destined to exhaust itself once it reaches an extrinsic goal:

> And since in some cases it is the exercise that is final (for example, seeing in the case of sight, and nothing different in addition to this comes to be from sight), but from others there does come to be something (for example, from the building craft a house in addition to the act of building), it is nevertheless in the one case no less the end, in the other more the end than the potentiality... In all the other cases where there is no other product in addition to the actuality, the actuality is in them (for example, seeing in the one seeing and contemplation in the one contemplating and living in the soul...).[19]

The acts which keep executing the potentiality of the musical score are actions; the ones which abandon the potentiality as premise, reaching a different goal than the exercise of a faculty, are rather *kinesis*, simple movement. The speaker, whose repertoire is limited to his ability to speak, never leaves it. He stages it, he makes it resonate, and he tests it, without proceeding toward something else. This is why the speaker doesn't effectuate a movement, but an action.

The speaker's paradoxical script is the power to speak, from which the existence of any other script depends. However, we need to distinguish two different kinds of potential scripts: the historico-natural language, and the linguistic faculty. The speech act (the Saussurian parole), as virtuoso performance, executes both in unison, but they are nevertheless two different kinds of *dynamis*. The historical language, marked by social and cultural vicissitudes, constitutes an infinite repertoire of potential speech acts: we should consider, for instance, the whole set of love declarations that we could compose with the specific Italian or Turkish phonetic, lexical and grammatical systems. The language faculty, instead, as biological endowment common to the entire species, does not correspond at all to a class (no matter how indefinite and extended) of eventual enunciations, but to the simple ability to enunciate. The historical language nearly anticipates, in both form and content, the concrete actions that the speaker can perform, while the faculty itself is formless, and empty of content: it is an indeterminate power, always heterogeneous to any specifiable action.

The execution of the script as historical language coagulates in the semantic content of our enunciations, in their communicative message: in short, in *what we say*. On the contrary, the script as faculty is visible in the action of speaking and of breaking the silence, that is, in *the fact of speech* (*infra*, ch.2). The two scripts of the linguistic animal as performer are always contemporaneous and inseparable. In the actual speech act, however, one or the other script can assume a greater visibility. The script as historical language is more dominant every time that the attention is drawn to the communicative message of the enunciation. But there are times when what we say has no importance whatsoever and what is decisive is the simple fact of speaking, of showing ourselves to others as an agent of speech. When we communicate that we are communicating (when what really counts is the act of enunciating and not the text of the enunciation) it is literally true that our "ultimate goal is the simple exercise of the faculty."

7. On theater: the stage and the quotation marks

The performing art closest to the common speech experience is undoubtedly the theater. In the actor's labor coexist, juxtaposed and sometimes indistinguishable, the specific virtuosity required by the acting stage and the universal virtuosity that pervades the entire linguistic praxis of *Homo sapiens*. The actor reproduces, in a closed environment and with the help of specialized techniques, the actions performed by every speaker, that is, by every man of action: he becomes visible to his fellow humans.

The actor acts by speaking. But those who act by speaking, are they all actors? This question is not as frivolous as one might first think. Rather than considering only the actor's performance from the perspective of every day speech, we also need to proceed in the opposite direction and to suppose that the staging of a play can help in clarifying some complicated issues pertaining to the philosophy of language. What we need to consider, in short, is the theatricality inherent to all speech, no matter how sloppy or clumsy. Besides being an empirically determined art, the theater might constitute an *a priori* form structuring and determining the entirety of our verbal activity. Among the many theatrical notions that might aspire to become guiding concepts in a reflection about language as praxis, I will only mention two: *a*) the existence of a *scene*, that is, of a determined area that insures the full visibility to the represented events; *b*) the *quotation marks* that contain all that is said during the performance. Both scene and quotation marks are indispensable elements of all human actions, and not some expedient invented to imitate them for a paying public.

a) For all of his gestures (a kiss or a treacherous stabbing) and words (disconsolate monologues or witty seductions), the actor benefits from a space where they are both always visible. This space is the scene. In it, there is no room for the discretion of mental representations. All that happens appears under a glaring light. The stage and the curtains are the transcendental presupposition of all drama or comedy, the condition for its development. The scene constitutes the phenomenon of the actor, since it makes him *appear*. This is why it presents us with a humble but effective solution to the crucial problem of Husserl's phenomenology: to separate the specific visible entity from visibility as such, or the content of a phenomenon from the revealing *phainestai* that makes it such. The space where the representation takes place does not coincide with the sum of events and speeches that occur there, but instead is the prerequisite that guarantees their revelation. The actor's replies attract the eye, but the appearance of all that appears is instituted by the scene.

In common linguistic practice, the theatrical stage is replaced by the *enunciation,* but only if we retain this term in the definition given by Benveniste when he says that "our object is not the text of the utterance, but the very act of producing the utterance."[20] The scene used by those who act verbally is simply the speech act. The speaker's visibility depends from the "individual conversion of language into speech"[21] and not from the latter's content or specific modalities. What discloses the space of appearance, where all event is given the status of phenomenon, is the passage from the pure power to speak ("before the enunciation the language is only the possibility of language"[22]) to the emissions of a signifying voice. The act of enunciating, the passage from potentiality to action, is marked by certain strategic words: the deictics "I," "this," "here," "now." According to Benveniste, those little words only refer to the "speech situation" created by them.[23] "I" is the one who is speaking, no matter what he or she might be saying; it is, in a way, the actor as separate from the character. "Here" and "now" denote the place and time of the enunciation, the place and time of the performance. "This" refers to what surrounds the speaker under the stage lights. The enunciation "introduces somebody who speaks via his or her own speech (parole),"[24] that is, to the role he's about to play.

In her essay "The *Vita Activa* and the Modern Age," Hannah Arendt underscores two traits characteristic of human praxis: the beginning of something new, nondetermined by any chain of events, and the revelation of oneself to other human beings. A contingent and unexpected incipit, similar to a second birth, is what constitutes the action in the purest sense, while in the speech that accounts for what the acting subject has done we find the roots of a revealing self-exhibition.[25] But if we consider them closely, we see that *both* of these aspects are already present in the linguistic experience, as long as we distinguish, with Benveniste, the act of enunciating from the text of the enunciation (or, as we said earlier, the "scene" from the "play"). All speakers set forth, each time anew, a unique and unrepeatable event. To use Arendt's concepts, we could say that the act of breaking the silence is the beginning of revelation. The sheer fact of enunciating, by itself without content, already insures to the speaker a maximum of visibility to all he or she will do or say: not only to his well-nuanced tales, but also to his mute gestures.

b) When the actor confesses a terrible secret, insults an unfaithful lover or describes a storm, his words resemble quotations. He does not really use those words, he mentions them. When proffered on a stage, the replies of a dialogue are always in quotation marks. What's more, this would be true also if they did not belong to a literary work but were the result of the wildest of improvisations. It is the stage *as such* that deprives these sentences of their usual function. Quotation marks express the relation between the space of appearance (the stage and the curtain) and what happens there (the play), between the transcendental conditions of representation and the events represented, between the act of speaking and a particular communicative message. It is clear, however, that this relation surpasses the restricted milieu of the theater and characterizes instead verbal praxis in general.

It is not by chance that Gottlob Frege refers to poetry when clarifying the status of those enunciations which, although possessing an intersubjective sense (*Sinn*), are nonetheless devoid of a verifiable meaning (*Bedeutung*). One example will suffice: "The sentence 'Odysseus was set ashore in Ithaca while sound asleep' obviously has a sense. But since it is doubtful whether the name 'Odysseus,' occurring therein, means anything, it is also doubtful whether the whole sentence does."[26] Where there is no search for truth, that is, a prevalent interest in the univocal correspondence between words and things, our enunciations are theatrical figures, they are *Sinn* without *Bedeutung*, texts enclosed in quotation marks. Husserl's assessment of "expressions without meaning," that is, enunciations without an informative value, is not very different: when we use them, "the hearer intuitively takes the speaker to be a person who is expressing this or that."[27] But presenting ourselves as speakers, doesn't it really mean to put ourselves on a stage, reciting our own sentences as the lines of a script? And this theatrical exhibition, doesn't it imply the passage from the actual use of an enunciation to its simple mention?

To determine whether the use of quotation marks is an exception, like Frege and Husserl seem to believe, or a fundamental trait of human speech, we should proceed backward, that is, asking in which cases we could do away with these embarrassing graphic markers. Our enunciations cease to be theatrical figures on two interrelated conditions: the first consists in emphasizing only the cognitive function of language, temporarily obscuring its true nature as praxis; the second resides in the separation of what we say (the semantic content) from the speech act (the enunciation), that is, in postulating the autonomy of the "play" with respect to any "scene." But these are the truly exceptional and artificial conditions. Verbal language is first and foremost action, *praxis*, and only in a second and derivative way can it function as *episteme*. From another perspective, the text of an enunciation always refers back to the act that produces it, just as the theatrical performance always presupposes a scene and a backstage. *What is anomalous, or at least ephemeral and reversible, is the absence of quotation marks.*

Linguistic activity is not defined by the extrinsic aims that it may happen to pursue, nor, let us be clear, by the goal of increasing our scientific knowledge. Suppressing the quotation marks is no different from emphasizing this or that occasional purpose for our speech acts, but maintaining them, and recognizing their original nature, means to remain faithful to language's actual functioning. The quotation marks signal, in fact, the natural arbitrariness of linguistic rules and the consequent inseparability of means and end, execution and result, use and mention. The theatricality of human verbal praxis is not exceptional, but radical constitutive and insuppressible. If we consider them on their own, as something that concerns our "living well in general," our enunciations are always "figures" according to Frege's definition, *Sinn* unencumbered by *Bedeutung*. And the speakers-actors, no matter what they say, never fail to be perceived as people who are "expressing this or that."

8. Linguistic animal, political animal

Let us summarize: the performance of the dancer or the violinist is an activity without a product, it lacks an external goal, and it necessarily implies the presence of others. These essential characteristics are also true of verbal action and ethico-political praxis. More importantly, language and the care for common affairs are in fact the matrix, the universal prototype of any activity without a product. The virtuosity of the technician, the musician or the dancer are simple illustrations, and in fact in an incomplete and artificial way, the fundamental and natural virtuosity always shown by the human animal engaged in the "potential space" between mind and world. However, the performing artist has a great merit: since he simultaneously recalls the speaker's abilities and the prudence (*phronesis*) of those who act in the public sphere, his or her performance is a precious link between the two famous definitions of *Homo sapiens* given by Aristotle: "animal with language" and "political animal."

These definitions don't pose any problem until we play with the idea that the second is subordinate, or at most complementary, to the first one. But they become far less innocuous when we understand them as fully synonymous and therefore tautological when we put them next to each other. The authors who have conceived language as production (*poiesis*) or cognition (*episteme*), as social instrument or internal patrimony of the mind, freely admit that the linguistic animal can at times also be political. But they never suspect, not even for a minute, that the two definitions are coextensive, inseparable and logically equivalent. Instead of lazily opining on the political uses of speech, we need to focus on the intrinsically political nature of language. This becomes clear as soon as we recognize the strong kinship between the speaker and the performing artist, or rather, as soon as we understand that articulate speech is first and foremost a virtuoso practice whose ultimate goal is the exercise of the faculty itself.

Politics is not a form of life among many, tied to a specific language game, as is believed by some excessively prudent Wittgensteinian thinkers. It does not find its roots in a circumscribed region of verbal activity, but is inherent to the very fact of *having* language. The biological configuration that allows us to speak and to act politically is one and the same. If anything, the political inclination of human speech constitutes the one presupposition for all different forms of life and language games (among which, of course, the cognitive and productive ones stand out for their importance). The study of language as biological organ of public praxis is not a marginal task that we could attend to during our leisure time, when the real work has been done, but the crux of every inquest on human nature. This kind of study looks at the foundations, not at the furnishings, and is situated at the same level of Chomsky's research on a universal grammar or Saussure's reflection on the double nature of the sign. It has nothing to do, on the other hand, with Chomsky's (admirable, but unrelated to its linguistic theories) anarchist militancy, and even less with the cheesy inanities typical of the sociology of communication. The linguistic animal is in itself political, with no further addition. All the rest is important of course, but only in the second instance. As a famous French general once said, *l'intendance suivra.*[28]

2

The Absolute Performative

1. What we say and the fact of speaking

In every enunciation there are two fundamental, symbiotic but distinctive aspects: a) *what we say*, the semantic content expressed by the enunciation thanks to certain phonetic, lexical and syntactic characters; b) *the fact of speaking*, the decision to break the silence, the act of enunciating as such, the speaker's exposure to the eyes of others.

Saussure's image of a sheet of paper composed of two inseparable sides, each dependent on the other, is particularly useful in this context. But what constitutes, precisely, the *recto* and *verso* sides of the sheets? What-we-say comprises in itself the whole relation between langue and parole, between the expressive opportunities offered by the system of a natural-historical language and their selective realization in a concrete speech act. The fact-of-speaking, instead, brings us back to the third pole of our linguistic experience, hastily individuated by Saussure: the *faculté de langage*, or the generic ability to speak, which is independent from any particular language. We know that Saussure, after mentioning it at the beginning of the *Course*, excludes this faculty from his scientific project, considering it an inextricable heap of physiological and biological elements.[1] By doing so, however, he refuses to examine closely what in human elocution is pure *dynamis*, both power and potentiality. This purely *potential*—and *biological*—side of language distinguishes it from the natural-historical languages. While a language still belongs to the realm of actuality, since it resides in an indefinite set of eventual acts (eventual because not yet executed, but nonetheless acts in form and content), the *faculté* is empty power-to-say, never equivalent to a series of hypothetical executions. The fact-of-speaking cannot be reduced either to the communicative act that is taking place (the *parole*), or to its virtual prefiguration within the *langue as system*: rather, it shows by means of a single enunciation that we have the *ability* to speak, the *power* to say something. The decision to speak, inseparable from a certain *dictum*, always exhibits a pure *sayability*, separate from any specific content. Ability on one side, language and enunciation on the other: these are the two inseparable sides of the same page.

It is not hard to recognize that many crucial—or at least grandiose—philosophical pairs find their humble material foundation in the two sides of the enunciation: the *empirical* what-we-say (even when we speak of teeth-grinding demons, the text of an enunciation is an object limited to a certain space-time), and the *transcendental* fact-of-speaking (the condition of possibility for any specific text). The first is *ontic* in nature (the particular product of our linguistic competence), while the second is *ontological* (since it proves the very existence of that competence). In addition, each of these two aspects emphasizes a different relation to the world. What-we-say represents or institutes worldly state of affairs: "the morning star is in fact the planet Venus," "I love you," "that rock is so sharp that it hurts my eyes," and so on. The fact-of-speaking, instead, shows language's insertion into the world as context or background for all states of things and enunciations. Paraphrasing Wittgenstein's famous distinction, we could say: the action of enunciating indicates *that* the world is in the moment when it inscribes itself in it.[2]

But the double character of the enunciation also implies a second conceptual bifurcation, less lofty than the previous one but perhaps not completely negligible. While what-we-say deploys the cognitive-communicative aspect of human language, the fact-of-speech shows its *ritual* character. We are not referring to an accidental kind of rituality, which only irrupts into certain specific occasions and then quickly evaporates, but to the ritual bent of *all* discourse. This does not concern only the words attached to a certain rite, but the rituality of any speech situation. The *recto* and *verso* sides of Saussure's page can also be represented in the following way: cognitive/ritual. As there is no specific text (what-we-say) that can be separated from the act of producing it (the fact-of-speaking), so there is no cognitive and communicative feat exempt from a ritual denotation.

We are not proposing, of course, to apply to language one of the established definitions of the rite, but, on the very contrary, to discern in the fact-of-speaking the very essence of rituality. All single ritual acts (including false contracts or horserace bets) are such precisely and only because we engage in speaking. It could be said that rituality often depends mostly on what-we-say, and therefore on specific contents of enunciation. This is certainly true, but in these cases it is easy to observe that what-we-say always refers to the fact-of-speaking, and that the specific enunciative contents are either limited to the cognitive elaboration of the enunciative act or derive from it symbolic value and all sorts of operational consequences. In their text, strictly ritual enunciations articulate in the most different ways the very "fact" that we are producing a text. This is the general foundation of rituality, and it includes also those enunciations that are decidedly *not* ritual, for instance the scientific ones.

The fact-of-speaking both founds and shows the ritual character of our speech. But if this is the case, what do we mean by "rite"? What is its most pertinent definition? As we know, the fact-of-speaking refers to a *faculté de langage* imbued with biological and physiological elements. In other words, it bears witness to the generic power to speak via a single, semantically determined *dictum*. We could then say that a rite always celebrates the distinction between faculty and act, language and speech. Since language, as separate from natural and historic languages, only exists as biological *dynamis*, we could also say that a rite underscores the difference between power and action in a specific linguistic act. We call "ritual," then, the empirical experience of transcendence, the discursive evocation of the biological disposition underlying all human speech. This is the objective texture of rite, or at least some of the threads running through it. It is clear, however, that we need to pay great attention to what happens to the officiating subject, since rite is a praxis, and not a conceptual inquiry. The production of an enunciation (not its text) allows the speaker to manifest herself, it literally makes her visible. "Speak, so that I might see you," wrote Lichtenberg in his fragment *On Physiognomy*, quoting an ancient sentence originally attributed to Socrates. With the simple emission of an articulated voice—or by positioning herself on the threshold between language and speech, which amounts to the same thing—the speaker becomes a phenomenon, something to which we can attribute a *phainestai*, an appearance. S/he exposes herself to the others' eyes. And it is in this exposition that we find the unmistakable work of the rite.

2. Communicating communication

The most conspicuous side of the enunciation/sheet, the one that immediately captures our attention, is usually *what* we say. The fact that we are speaking, instead, most frequently remains unnoticed. Although it is part of every elocution, or maybe just because of this, this fact does not have an autonomous relevance. The fact-of-speaking is the unrecognized presupposition, the unseen background, of what-we-say. The speech act is in the service of the communicative message. There are, however, language games where the usual relation between back and foreground is inverted: language games where what really matters is the fact that we speak, while what we say dissolves, becoming a simple expedient or an ancillary message. We would like to analyze this inversion between recto and verso that allows for the semantic content to figure as a simple signal for the speech act, and for the enunciation to simply mean that we are enunciating something. In other words, we want to address some actual enunciations where the relation between *langue* and *parole* simply refers to the *faculté de langage*. Far from constituting a marginal anomaly, they give us the opportunity to address extremely important logical and ethical issues.

There are many techniques that insure that we forget, or bracket, the semantic content of the enunciation while stressing the simple fact that we are enunciating. The mechanical repetition of the same sentence (let's think about echolalia, for instance, that we find in all ordinary conversations, and not only in its childish or pathological manifestations) obscures—or should we rather say, sacrifices—the communicative message, leaving free reign to the event constituted by the speech act itself. This is also true for some stereotypical formulas, such as "*buongiorno*," or "How are you"? Think, for instance, about the so-called "phatic" function: the interlocutors don't say anything, if not that they are speaking ("Hello, hello," or "Yes, I'm here"), and they don't do anything, if not making themselves visible, exposing themselves to the others' eyes. In an essay devoted to primitive communities that is perfectly relevant to the digital chatter of the contemporary universe, Malinowski said: "Are words in phatic communication used primarily to convey meaning, the meaning which is symbolically theirs? Certainly not. They fulfil a social function and that is their principal aim."[3] The views expressed in such circumstances openly acknowledge their lack of grounding and their volatility. Rather than texts endowed with a specific value, they are *pre-texts* whose sole function is to draw attention to the fact of speaking as performed by a certain speaker.

The phatic function prevents any real exchange of information, interrupts or differs the propagation of a specific message and atrophies the descriptive use of language. The enunciation simply refers to the fact that someone produced it. It does not reflect a certain state of the world, but it configures an event. This event, however, is unique insofar as it simply consists in the insertion of discourse in the world. Malinowski adds that "it is obvious that the outer *situation* does not enter directly in the technique of speaking. But what can be considered a situation when a number of people aimlessly gossip together? [...] the whole situation consists in what happens linguistically."[4] The speech act reflects back on itself, content with its own completion, without boasting a specific object or a particular aim. Exposing oneself to the eyes of others requires as its optimal condition the rarefaction of messages. This is not, however, an absolute void: the absence of a specific and relevant *dictum* allows the communication of the generic communicability that founds every *dictum*.

The phatic function implicitly emphasizes the fact of speaking more than what we say. Let's ask ourselves whether it's possible to make explicit all that the phatic function—like other discursive forms that we will analyze later—accomplishes by stealth. In other words: is it possible to extract the fact of speaking, an essential aspect of every enunciation, and to express it in a separate utterance? Of course it's possible: we simply need to say: "*I speak.*"

3. What is an absolute performative?

John L. Austin calls performative enunciations such as "I take this woman as my wife," "I baptize this child Luca," "I swear I'll come to Rome," "I bet that Inter will win the championship." Those who say these words don't describe an action (a wedding, a baptism, a promise, a bet), they execute it. They don't talk about what they are doing, they do something by talking.

"I speak" also realizes an action through words. In fact, nothing else is signaled but the speaker's enunciating act. Therefore, we are faced with a true performative enunciation. Except that, in the specific case of "I speak," the action realized solely through words consists exclusively of... speaking. It is a performative, but an anomalous one, whose extreme nature is self-evident. Its more domesticated relatives, such as "I forgive you," or "I order you to leave," perform an action at the precise moment of their enunciation but, as Austin remarks, such action "is not to describe my doing of what I should be said in so uttering to be doing."[5] Saying something is the necessary *presupposition*, or the necessary *mean*, for forgiving, ordering, being married or baptizing somebody, but it is not the definitional content of such actions. In the case of "I speak," however, what we do in saying these words can't be described otherwise than by simply saying something. While "I forgive you" or "I order you to leave" are events produced through language, "I speak" only produces the *event of language*.

The enunciation "I speak" is the *absolute performative*. But *why* is it absolute?

First of all because, by saying it, we only realize the action—that is, the fact of speaking—constituting the hidden presupposition of all the normal performative sentences and that allows them to realize a specific action.

Secondly, because when I say "I speak," I express in a performative way, that is, without having recourse to metalinguistic affirmations, the act of textual production constituting one of the two aspects of every enunciation. "I speak" is an empty and indeterminate action, just like the fact-of-speaking taken separately from what-we-say. "I speak" is the performative act illuminating the general performativity of all enunciations.

Thirdly, because "I speak" is the only performative whose validity is not dependent on specific extra-linguistic conditions. Those who give commands or baptize have to be invested with certain institutional prerogatives; they must be, for instance, either generals or priests. This is not true for those who perform the act of speaking. But we will come back to this.

Finally, because only "I speak" is completely self-referential. Ordinary performatives mention the action accomplished through the enunciation, but they ignore the enunciation as such. The blind spot of self-referentiality is, in this case, the-fact-of-speaking. "I take this woman as my wife," instead, refers to its own enunciation as to the event produced by it. Not only does it perform an action, but mentions speaking only as the action it accomplishes.

"I speak" is the absolute performative. But we must admit that it occurs very rarely. There is something bizarre and unusual about it. At first sight, it seems that this kind of enunciation can only be appropriate in exceptional circumstances. What is the use, then, of such an extreme case? Why spend so much time on an anomaly? The fact is that only the absolute performative truly accounts for the innumerable linguistic forms where what-we-say recedes in the background while the-fact-of-speaking comes to the forefront. Coming back to what we said before, we see that the structure and function of the phatic function can only be understood in the light of the enunciation "I speak."

The absolute performative is the true logical form of all language games whose text unequivocally refers to the enunciation. From "I speak" we can recognize with absolute certainty the implicit performativity of these language games, which are pervasive and extremely relevant. Beyond phatic communication (which we used as an introductory example), the absolute performative thoroughly characterizes at least two essential fields: the egocentric language of children, a decisive ontogenetic step for the human animal, and religious language. More generally, the absolute performative operates when the ritualistic aspect of language comes to the fore. But before showing the concrete field of application of "I speak," we need to specify with more precision its internal statute.

4. The formal structure of the enunciation "I speak"

We need to add two marginal corollaries to what we just said. The first one concerns the notion, found in Austin, of "locutory act." The second one benefits from the analysis of the so-called "delocutive verbs" proposed by Emile Benveniste. Both aim uniquely at better illustrating the nature of the enunciation "I speak" and of its many implicit equivalents, although with variations in perspective.

In the absolute performative the locutory act—the humblest and most overlooked among the linguistic acts identified by Austin—comes into the foreground and assumes an essential role. It perfectly coincides with the simple action of constructing an enunciation: "to emit certain sounds, say certain words within a certain construction and with a certain 'meaning.'"[6]

Austin's uncontested merit resides in having considered even the simplest of signifying voice emissions as a true act, indeed as the act that can never be missing when we do something with words. However, Austin mentions the indispensable act of producing an enunciation only to emphasize, by contrast, the far more complex structure of the linguistic acts he truly considers important: "Our interest for the locutory act, naturally, is mostly directed at making clear what it is, so that we may distinguish it from the other acts on which we will focus most of our attention."[7] In sum, the "locutory act" figures as a *genus* so encompassing as to become no more than an accomplice. What is interesting are instead some slippery and paradoxical *species*, and the performative most of all. But when we say "I speak" the situation changes radically. This enunciation is unquestionably a performative, but one that only accomplishes a "locutory act" and refers to it while doing so. We could also say that the absolute performative is a locutory act that accounts for its own production. The *genus* (the simple emission of the signifying voice) becomes the object or the final objective of the *species* (performative). The most general of premises appears as a most pointed conclusion. The presupposition becomes the *terminus ad quem*.

With an original neologism, Emile Benveniste calls "delocutive" (that is, derived from an elocution) the verbs that do not come from the semantic content of a nominal syntagm, but from its actual elocution. Instead of taking their signification from their corresponding nouns, they designate the act of saying them: therefore, they refer us to a phonic enunciation. As an example, let's take the verb "to salute": it does not come from the Latin substantive *salus*, but it expresses the action consisting in saying Salus! Its true paraphrase, thus, is "to say

'*Salus!*'" Similarly, Benveniste remarks, to negate signifies saying '*nec*,' the French verb *tutoyer* means to say *tu*, and so on.[8]

Already in their formal structure, delocutive verbs operate with exemplary clarity a shift in emphasis between what we say and the fact of speaking: the relative inconsequence of the text accompanies the primacy attributed to the enunciatory act. As Benveniste writes, "the delocutive is defined not by the intentional content but by the formal relationship between a locution and a verb denoting the utterance of that locution."[9] This shift assimilates them to the verbs informing the most common performative enunciations, such as "to swear," "to order," "to baptize," etc. Like the performatives, they are "verbs denoting discursive activities" (Austin or Benveniste?) and refer to an actual locutory enunciation. Clearly, this does not imply that all delocutives have a purely performative function, although some do, as the already mentioned "to salute," whereby we perform an action by talking about it. What is really important is that performatives and delocutives share the constant logical form of "*to say: X*." To swear means "to say 'I swear,'" to baptize means "to say: I baptize you," just as to negate means "to say: *nec*," *tutoyer* "to say: *tu*" and so forth.

Against this kind of background, we can now see the contours of the absolute performative in its distinctive features. It brings to its most extreme consequences the hierarchical reversal between what we say and the fact of speaking. Only the second aspect survives: when we say "I speak" we only say that we have started speaking, the text limits itself to declaring that an enunciative act is under way. Delocutives and ordinary performatives still attribute a role, however diminished and indirect, to their semantic content: the latter survives as logical variant ("*Salus*!," "*I swear*," etcetera) destined to complete the constant "to say: X." The absolute performative, instead, adopts as variant nothing more than the logical constant itself. "I speak" only denotes the generic enunciatory act that is subtended in any other "discursive activity." The pure "to say," extracted from specifications such as "to swear," "to salute," "to negate," etcetera, surfaces again on the other side of the colon, constant and variable at the same time. And indeed, it is this compression that signifies the unbridled self-reflexivity of "I speak."

If the absolute performative could create a delocutive verb, its meaning would be "*to say: I say.*"

5. For voice only

The absolute performative rests on the emission of an articulated *sound.* It emphasizes the *physiological* traits of human speech. The *voice* becomes a conceptual determination, the *breath* a logical apex. If we consider this closely, we see that none of the usual performative enunciations can be thought of silently, or simply muttered away in the internal dialogue of the soul. If they want to be effective, sentences such as "I take this woman as my wedded wife," "I bet that Inter will end up in the B series," "I salute you," demand a complete and adequate vocalization. A phonic elocution is the necessary condition of every enunciation directed at performing a certain action all by itself. If "to swear" means "to say: I swear," those who accomplish this action have to produce a *flatus vocis*: only the latter, in fact, denotes the meaning of the first part of "I swear," that is "to say: X."

The absolute performative radicalizes the issue. In phatic communication (like in the egocentric language of the child and in religious communication, as we will see very soon), showing the fact of speaking is the true aim of the enunciation. But when separated from what we say and valorized as such, the fact of speaking only and entirely coalesces, so to speak, around the material emission of articulated sounds. This is why vocalization, in the case of the absolute performative, isn't only the necessary condition (like for "swearing," "saluting," "betting," etcetera) but also the primary *result* of the action. The action denoted by the expression "I speak" and its equivalents fully coincides with the *flatus vocis*. The most vulgar physiological aspect of speech comes to constitute the apex of linguistic communication, what is really at stake when we speak. The phonic performance becomes the aim of syntactic competence. However, while it is true that the absolute performative accounts for the event of language, of its insertion in the world, we need to specify that in doing so it depends fully on the occlusion and the distension of the breath. The event of language is contained in the work of the epiglottis: its insertion in the world flashes through an air movement. If it is true that "I speak" is purely self-referential, we still have to say that such self-referentiality lacks nothing, precisely because it proceeds from the biological foundations of speech.

The fact of speaking manifests the linguistic faculty, the indeterminate potential to say something, the distinctive language of the natural-historical languages. We know, though, that the linguistic faculty is a hybrid entity, marked by physiological and biological elements. This is why, within a well-defined enunciation, the generic faculty is only affirmed through the equally hybrid reality of the signifying *voice*. Let's be careful, though: the faculty is affirmed through a voice able to signify, not the specific meaning that it expresses. The simple production of articulated sounds illustrates both the potential and the physiological character of the linguistic faculty. With regard to the exceptional importance given to vocalization in the absolute performative, we think that a casual observation by Wittgenstein is appropriate: "the physiological symbolizes the logical."[10] The rhythm of the breath, the contractions of the diaphragm, the tongue pushing against the teeth (the physiological) represent at every time the power to speak (the logical).

All rituals are strictly tied to phonic elocution. Vocal emission is not only a suggestive addition to all kind of ceremonies (pledges, bets, pardons, etc.), but their very foundation. The voice is ritualistic because it symbolizes the linguistic faculty. Rite *illustrates*—in both senses of the word, as showing and honoring—the nexus between physiology and logics.

The ceremony of the voice, the occurrence of speech, makes the speaker visible as the bearer of the power to speak. Although inelegant, the word "bearer" is strategic. Frege has clarified several times that objective thought, unlike individual psychological representations, is independent of any "bearer": three plus two still makes five, even if nobody believes it or expresses it.[11] Instead, the enunciation "I am scared of snakes" is only true when it refers to the empirical subject suffering from such a phobia. This means that the linguistic faculty disrupts Frege's alternative since, while it has nothing to do with a psychological representation, it still needs an individual substratum, that is, an "owner." In fact, unlike actualities, potentials never have an autonomous existence: the fact of speech can never be separated from a living body. More universal than a natural language, the linguistic faculty is tied to the body of the single speaker. The voice is ritualistic because, by symbolizing the potential for speech, it insures the full exposure to the external eye of the particular living body imbued with such power. With its focus on the phonic emission, rituals administer both the fleeting *incarnation* of the linguistic faculty—of language as different from the different natural languages—and the *epiphany* of the biological entity constituting the speaker.

6. Rituality of language, ritual *as* language

Austin affirms that performatives, which are never false, can still be "*unhappy*."[12] The enunciation "I take this woman as my wedded wife" is condemned to be inappropriate, that is, to failure, if it is said in the wrong circumstances: for instance, if the speaker is bigamous, if it is just a joke, or if the bride is absent. Whether we have an abuse (the bigamous) or we misfire (the wedding formula is said while the bride leaves with another man), the fact is that the action to be realized through the words remains unexecuted. According to Austin, performative enunciations share the danger of being ineffective with all those actions having "a general character of ritual or ceremonial."[13] A voodoo ritual, pins in the enemy's effigies and all, is void when performed by a Diderot's devotee in front of his students as illustration of a primitive mentality. Infelicity is a concern for the whole class of ritual actions, linguistic or not.

Performatives, however, also suffer from a completely different affliction: their emptiness. Empty, that is, ineffective, is an enunciation such as "Tomorrow I will come to Rome" if it is inserted in a poem or used as a quotation. This second affliction, says Austin, lurks in every enunciation, performative or descriptive alike. "As *utterances* our performatives are also heir to certain kind of ills which affect *all* utterances."[14] To sum up: as part of the class of ritual actions, performatives risk being ineffective, while as part of the class of enunciations, they can become void. These are two different weaknesses, rooted in partially heterogeneous terrains.

It is easy to see how the absolute performative avoids both risks. Ineffectiveness can't touch it. If I say "I speak" (or one of its implicit equivalents), the action of speaking is always realized. Circumstances and social roles have no bearing on this action. Those who perform this linguistic act not only have the power to do so, but in fact act with the specific intent of showing it. The possibility of committing an abuse or of misfiring is by definition excluded. Furthermore, since we are simply expressing the fact that we are speaking, the absolute performative is also exempt from the dangers of being void. When the actor says the words "I speak" while he is performing on stage, he really executes the act of enunciating, just as completely and effectively as someone who is completely foreign to theatrical fictions and says the same words in some emotional circumstance tied to his daily life.

Why, then, are utterances emphasizing only the fact of speaking immune both from the weaknesses that can make rituals infelicitous (including ordinary performatives as rites), and those that can undermine all enunciations (including ordinary performatives as enunciations)? For the very good reason that the fact of speaking, as illustrated by the absolute performative, is the precondition for all utterances and rituals. Speech, the indispensable condition of all linguistic acts, is not touched by the dangers surrounding specific texts. Speech, the origin of the rituality typical of the human animal, can never be a fictitious rite. It knows no inappropriate circumstances, since it is itself the unavoidable "circumstance" of any particular ceremony. The ordinary performatives discussed by Austin run all the risks of rituals and enunciations alike because they are tied at least in part to what is said. Either they institute a ritual through a specific enunciation, or they execute an enunciation that also has a certain ritual value. The absolute performative, instead, avoids such dangers because it limits itself to the celebration of the foundational rite of language. The absolute performative makes visible both *the rituality of language* and the *linguistic nature of rituals*.

7. Re-enacting anthropogenesis

Even having excluded ineffectiveness and vacuity, we still need to ask what could be the possible "deficiency" of the absolute performative. A probable answer might be the following: although never void or ineffective, the absolute performative can be redundant, pleonastic, *superfluous*.

It is obvious that we don't always feel the need to privilege the fact of speaking as such, and that only rarely are we prepared to downplay what we say reducing it to signal the mere act of enunciation. Phatic communication ("Hello! Hello, I'm here!), where the speaker simply proclaims that he has started to speak, often appears corny and oppressive. Similarly, mystic talk (the sublime version of "Hello, I'm here"!) can sometime inspire the same dislike ordinarily reserved to overwrought tautologies, since it only shows *the event of language*. The metaphysical tradition is a perfect example of the redundant and pleonastic nature of the absolute performative "I speak": in this case, however, such redundancies—far from being considered dangerous—are proudly assumed as great virtues. Let's take Hegel, for example. In his *Phenomenology of the Mind* we can see that what we say is incessantly *sacrificed*: if at the beginning the content of speech claims all the rights of our multifaceted concrete reality, later it reveals its nothingness (the "work of negativity"), diminishes and ultimately vanishes to the point of coinciding with the fact of speaking, its one unquestionable truth. Starting with the very first chapter, devoted to the deictics "this" and "I," and ending with its last pages on the linguistic community of the believers, the act of enunciating is continuously opposed to the contingent and inessential text of the enunciation.

The absolute performative can be redundant and superfluous (or even worse, omnivorous). This is its typical affliction. This affirmation, however, forces us to indicate at least summarily in what occasions it is appropriate, or even necessary and beneficial. When do we feel the need to emphasize the fact that we are going to speak? Why, from time to time, do we feel obliged to bear witness to our own ability to speak? What is the ritual action accomplished through the sentence "I speak," matrix and foundation of all rituals? Or, to put it more simply: what is the purpose of the absolute performative?

Staging the fact of speech is appropriate—and actually desirable—every time our lived experience is forced to retrace the essential steps of our becoming human. That is, every time that a danger, a doubt, a possible confusion can be dispelled only by reenacting, within the specific forms of human life, the travails of *anthropogenesis*. The recourse to the absolute performative has an apotropaic, protective function, because it allows such a reenactment. "I speak" provides us with the ritual reaffirmation of the differential characteristics of the *Homo sapiens* in a concrete historical or biographical conjuncture. Anthropogenesis becomes synchronic to the most different, and maybe even complicit, empirical circumstances. By emphasizing the fact of speech as mere faculty, we go once more through the threshold crossed by our species *in illo tempore* (and by the individual in his or her infancy). Let's take the case of self-awareness. In certain situations the "syntactic unit of apperception" vacillates and regresses, revealing itself to be not an unconditional presupposition but a problematic (and partially reversible) result. In these cases, the absolute performative is indeed appropriate and is enunciated *at the right time*: it is not pleonastic, but indispensable. Those who emphasize the fact of speaking over semantic content repeat a crucial step in the process leading to self-awareness: to represent oneself as a speaking being while speaking. The absolute performative, making ourselves visible as "bearers" of the linguistic faculty, can either reintroduce or confirm the "transcendental unit" of the I that for a moment appeared compromised or impaired.

To resume, we can say that "I speak" is never redundant when it contributes to overcome indecisions and crises serious enough to threaten the very presuppositions that generally help us to overcome all indecisions and crises. The language games celebrating the enunciatory act over what is said are perspicuous and salutary in all those situations when, in order to solve an empirical problem, we need to reassess the relation between the empirical and the transcendent, between experience and presuppositions, between fore- and background. The absolute performative ritually represents and reiterates the crucial steps of the anthropogenesis. In the course of an everyday, banal conversation, it allows the speaker to retrace his or her own genetic steps, and to go back for a moment to what made him or her... a speaker. On the individual biological level, a speech whose logic form is "to say: 'I say'" implies traveling back to our infancy. In other words, it delineates a sudden back turn on the road to ontogenesis.

8. Egocentric language

The enunciations where an adult emphasizes the fact of speech, focusing on his or her own linguistic faculty, find a decisive precedent (and sometimes even a detailed formal model) in the egocentric language of children. This is the real ontogenetic episode that will later be reenacted and repeated with apotropaic intentions. In the case of the beginning speaker, the absolute performative is not confined to reinstate or confirm self-awareness, but institutes it.

The notion of "egocentric language" has been introduced by Jean Piaget in 1923 and furthered by Lev S. Vygotsky in 1934.

Between three and six years of age, the child often creates an *external monologue*. It is a monologue because the child is talking to her or himself, turning away from intersubjective communication. It is external because this solitary speech is enunciated out loud, and in public. The child is speaking only for him or herself, but in the presence of others. The first kind of egocentric language is *echolalia*, that is, the repetition of sentences that the child has just heard, the exact or modified repetition of syllables and sounds. We play with language, diverting it from any finalized aim: "the child enjoys repeating the words for their own sake, for the pleasure they give him, without any external adaptation and without an audience."[15] Secondly, we have *fabulation*, which "consists in creating reality through language"[16]: the emission of articulated sounds assumes, in this case, a properly *magic* value, as it is supposed to act on the surrounding world without having without having any contact with things or persons. A third kind of linguistic egocentrism consists in verbally *announcing* what we are doing or we want to do. In this case, "words only serve as stimuli, not as communication"[17]: the verbal indication of the act being executed is also an act aimed at boosting the confidence of the speaker.

Cognitive scholars have systematically misunderstood the linguistic performances of children. They only take into consideration the text of the enunciations, their semantic content, the learning process or the intentional projects that they supposedly manifest. What they don't understand is that the stakes of egocentric language do not reside in what we say, but in the fact of speaking. We can even say that the different kinds of self-directed speech isolate in its purest form what Benveniste calls "the formal apparatus of enunciation": the apparatus is in fact speech itself. What do echolalia, the ludic attitude towards words, the appreciation for the material reality of syllables and sounds indicate, if not a marked indifference toward the message expressed and the corresponding preference for repeatedly experimenting with the *factum loquendi*, that is, with the insertion of language into the world? Similarly, the magic power of fabulation resides in the emission of articulated sounds, not in their meaning. The spell able to modify reality is the voice, its rhythm, the magnetic litany that it creates. The child, when verbally announcing what he or she is doing, is not describing an action, but completes a secondary, auxiliary action (the production of an enunciation), whose goal is the visibility of its subject.

In egocentric language, we experiment with a double suspension: a suspension of communication as chain of signals and counter-signals, of stimuli and responses; a suspension of the biunivocal nexus between words and things and therefore of the denotative function. Through this eclipse, the self-reflexive I is born. Self-awareness emerges thanks to a detachment, it prospers in a vacuum, it is a concave space. Their soliloquies allow children to experience him or herself as source of enunciations. In the theatrical rites of echolalia and fabulation he succeeds in representing himself as speaker. All the sentences without object and without an interlocutor aim at designating the ability to produce speech and its bearer. What is expressed by "I speak?"? Nothing more than "I speak." But "I speak" is both the foundation and the goal of self-reflection.

It is true, of course, that when we address our selves we also face cognitive problems such as avoiding an obstacle, solving a problem and so forth. But the point is that the child can do so only once he or she has become visible as source of enunciations, as bearer of the signifying voice. This visibility derives from a ritual practice (the exhibition of speech), not from a cognitive strategy. We will give a single, unassailable proof for this affirmation. According to Piaget and Vygotsky egocentric language often appears as collective monologue: many children are together, with each one only talking to him or herself but still attributing a great importance to the presence of the others. We can see that this is not that different from the prayers of the Christian mass. The presence of others is important because each monologue needs witnesses who, although they understand nothing of what is said, nonetheless take note of the fact of speech. The absolute performative finds its ideal home in this kind of collective monologue.

9. The principle of individuation

Vygotsky differs from Piaget in that he believes that the child's egocentric language is not the first ambiguous and contradictory step toward a progressive socialization. On the contrary, he thinks that its role consists in *singularizing* the speaker, emancipating him or her from an original pre-individual and communal condition. While for Piaget the external monologue stems from the insufficient socialization of an initially individual language, Vygotsky retraces its origin to "the insufficient individualization of primary social speech."[18] According to the Russian psychologist, the child's monologue is a bridge between the impersonal pronoun "we," or "one" ("we" think or "one" thinks, "we" do or "one" does, "we" believe or "one" believes) and the singular "I." In other words, it marks the transition from *inter*psychic—which are rooted in the collective activities of the child—to *intra*psychic connections and the eventual constitution of a well differentiated Self.[19] Vygotsky's perspective allows a grand restaging of the old question concerning *the principle of individuation*. Instead of being an absolute beginning, the individual becomes an end product. But how does the detachment from the impersonal "we" occur? What constitutes the *principium individuationis*?

Maternal language is pre-individual: it belongs to everyone and no one; it is a public and collective dimension. It shows with great clarity the preliminary sociality of the speaker. Egocentric language individuates (actually, it is the very principle of individuation) precisely because it allows us to detach ourselves from our language in the only possible way: emphasizing the generic ability to speak, that is, the biological-potential grounding of any natural-historical language. Let's take, for instance, the experience of the translator. The passage from English to Italian occurs in a no-man's land, or rather, thanks to the empty linguistic ability, separate from any single language. Although it has no autonomous reality (differently from what is actually there) the faculty can still be experienced in the *transition* from a language to another. Like self-awareness, the indeterminate ability to speak is a concave space, or a negative residue, not an independent protuberance. In the external monologue, the child behaves as a translator, not because he passes to a different natural-historical language, but because he or she becomes familiar with the precondition that makes such a passage possible: the partial detachment from the impersonal amniotic liquid of the maternal language and the manifestation of the linguistic faculty. It is thanks to that detachment and that ability that the speaker can achieve his or her own *individuation*.

Let's go back to a question that we had mentioned earlier. The de-activation of the communicative and referential functions allows the child's monologues to focus on the action of speaking. This is when the child *knows* that he or she is speaking. This "knowing that we are speaking" is initially expressed with a special kind of speech, a soliloquy pronounced out loud. In these soliloquies, the child *represents him or herself as speaker*. Representing oneself as speaker clearly implies belonging to a certain natural-historic language, but it does not end there. And in fact, such a representation, insofar as it presupposes the eclipse of the communicative function, finds its main support on the action of speaking, which surpasses by far the limits of any single language. In the external monologue, the child isolates, tests and exhibits his or her own speaking *potential*: this is why he or she starts many sentences without finishing them, or plays and distorts words, often becoming incomprehensible. In these speaking acts, the child does not perform a univocal representation of the natural language, but attests to a generic faculty as ontological proof of the power to speak. This attestation consists in the emission of articulated sounds. The ontological proof of the power to speak is given by the signifying voice. Therefore, the speech act aimed at testing and proving has to be understood as a physiological performance, as rhythmic breathing. In egocentric language, there is a separation between language and speech act: the natural language that ordinarily subtends the linguistic faculty without any residue, loses its preeminence and becomes a simple intermediary between those two other poles. Indicating in parentheses the term that, while being fully operative, is either implicit or remains in the background, we could say the child's soliloquies are represented by the following formula: faculty/(natural language)/ speech act. Ordinary language, instead, has to be represented thus: (faculty)/natural language/speech act.

The practice of external monologue allows the human being to draw attention on a previously invisible linguistic ability. This is how we can distance ourselves from our maternal language and its pre-individual, "interpsychic" character. But why would the experience of the power to speak afford us an unequivocal singularity? How does the passage from natural-historic language to the linguistic faculty realize the speaker's individuation? If historical-natural languages are the anonymous patrimony of a particular community, the linguistic faculty belongs to the entire species: far from diminishing, its universality is incommensurably bigger. But it is the increased universality of the power to speak that has the counter-effect of allowing us to circumscribe the speaker's singularity. In order to find the precise point of individuation, we need to push much deeper into the recesses of the generic and of the common.

Let's try to unravel this apparent paradox. Historic-natural languages are and remain pre-individual, because they exist independently from the single speaker: they are consigned to dictionaries, literary texts, grammars, wordplays, rhetorical figures and so on. Like a mathematical proposition, it does not depend on any particular "bearer." With the linguistic faculty, however, things change. As we have already seen, the power to speak, since it has no objective reality, is attached to a concrete, living body, and is undistinguishable from a single organism. Differently from a natural-historic language (which is a system of eventual acts, and not a potential), the linguistic faculty does not exist separately from one or another contingent speaker. It is true that the entire species shares this faculty, but since it is a potentiality, it is only shared as far as each of its members assumes and incarnates it. Or rather: more than incarnating it individually, each member of the species becomes an individual thanks to this incarnation. The power to speak is the personal experience constituting each and every person.

Speakers achieve their singularity when the importance of what is said is weakened or erased and they can represent themselves as specific bearers of a biological-linguistic *dynamis*. This is what happens in the child's external monologue: as we have seen, the fact of speaking, the inauguration of the signifying voice, the enunciating act comes to the fore. Infantile soliloquies individuate the speaker, but they can only do so because its logic form is "I speak," which is to say that it is the equivalent of the absolute performative. The singularity instituted by a self-representation as bearer of the linguistic faculty, of course, is still an empty one. We will fill it up progressively with all that we will say about ourselves: biographical vicissitudes, embarrassing anecdotes, short-lived triumphs and so forth. But it would be a mistake to attribute our individuation to the factual contents of our monologues. These contents acquire a great interest only because they are referred to someone who, having already said "I speak," has already affirmed his or her singularity. Only those who have already claimed the indeterminate power to speak, becoming the singular substratum of any particular attribution and therefore already formally individuated, can be responsible *for their own* biographies.

10. Vygotsky's error

Vygotsky says that the child's egocentric language is the laboratory for the creation of the kind of verbal thought traditionally called "internal language." Egocentric enunciations are amphibious: extroverted in structure and execution, they already perform the typical functions of silent meditation. They characterize the short intervals when the internal dialogue of the soul is still audible. Very soon, egocentrism will lose its dignity, becoming muffled and imperceptible. Criticizing Piaget, Vygotsky says that it is a mistake to consider the child's external soliloquies useless residues, without a future legacy: on the contrary, they are destined to become *internal* monologues, that is, thoughts constituted by non-uttered words. But can we believe in this legacy? Is it really true that the essential traits of egocentric language are absorbed into silent verbal thought? I believe that in this matter Vygotsky is patently wrong.

In the internal monologue of the adult, certain cognitive peculiarities of egocentric language are in fact prolonged and refined: first of all, the progressive symbiosis between words and thoughts, that is, the fact that we think *with* words.[20] This is a lot, but not all. There is an important and actually essential part of infantile thought that cannot be transformed into "internal language." This is, in fact, the part that determines the constitution and the self-awareness of the speaker: the emphasis put on the fact of speech (or on the action of enunciation), the privileging of the ability to speak over what we are saying, our direct relation with the linguistic faculty. All these aspects are rooted in the voice, in phonic emission, in the air movement produced by our mouths and lungs. Vocalization is not a secondary aspect of egocentric language: its elimination alters and weakens the general meaning of this phenomenon. It is to the vocal emission that are tied both the performativity and the rituality of the child's self-directed speech. This monologue always says "I speak": the only action it executes is the instantiation of speech itself. This action, however, would not be realized if the "I speak" were not said out loud. To resume: audible egocentric speech is entrusted with the absolute performative, but the same cannot be said about its presumed sole heir, that is, "internal language." Furthermore, the voice attributes a ritual value to the instantiation of speech, making the speaker visible as bearer of the linguistic faculty: visible to others, of course, but also to him or herself. The extrinsic soliloquies of the child, and not the later internal monologue, shows the ironclad connection between the fact of speech and the ritual behavior of the human animal, that is, the rituality of language and the linguistic nature of rituals.

Egocentric language is a composite model, and only a few of its elements survive in the "internal language" of the adult. Other essential elements follow instead a completely different path. Vygostky's mistake is to disregard as meaningless those traits of infantile monologue that are not assumed by verbal thought. He neglects the *logic* role of the voice (which guarantees the self-reference of those enunciating whose meaning is "I speaking") as well as its *ritual* nature. Far from weakening and disappearing, what is not transferred to the internal monologue of the adult survives in many *vocalized* performances of the older speaker. Or rather: it reappears in a much evolved form in all of those instances when what we say only serves to denote the fact of speech. The legal heirs of infantile soliloquy are those enunciations that embody, implicitly or explicitly, the absolute performative, like, for instance, in the *collective monologues* staged by phatic communication or religious ceremonies.

The most direct continuation of early egocentric speech are the soliloquies that the adult speakers sometimes allow themselves in a rather theatrical or apotropaic vein. Whether in the street or in a closed room, otherwise perfectly normal adults can direct to themselves an admonition or an injunction, a request or an exhortation. In well-articulated sounds, he or she might exclaim "Go back" or "Stay calm," or maybe "What did I do to deserve this?," "Stop it," "That's what I'll do," or "I can't believe it!" All these sentences don't have a well-defined semantic content: a hidden listener would not be able to identify their referent and their communicative message. They are more than a simple emotional outburst since the speaker addresses him or herself and tries to act through these words. On the other hand they are less than a self-standing enunciation since what is said is either incomprehensible or irrelevant. To keep things simple, let's admit that the meaning of the audible sentences enunciated by a solitary adult speaker depend from previous silent reflections: we would still have to ask why, at a certain moment, verbal thought abandons its habitual silence and becomes once again external monologue or, if we want, noisy egocentric language. Why should we pronounce out loud admonitions and exhortations that could be formulated more discretely in an inconspicuous "internal language"?

On this question, it is interesting to read the analysis of Edmund Husserl in one of his *Logical Investigations*, called Expression and Meaning. The eighth paragraph is entitled "Expressions in solitary life."[21] What does the solitary speaker *do*? Nothing, according to Husserl, that could be subsumed under what we normally mean as "speech." The speaker is *not even* communicating with him or herself. The uttered sentences certainly don't mean to inform the speaker of "indicating the existence of mental acts." The author of the soliloquy doesn't need to be told what he or she is feeling: "In a monologue, words can perform no function of indicating the existence of mental acts, since such indication would there be quite purposeless. For the acts in question are themselves experienced by us at that very moment."[22] Self-directed enunciations are unabashedly superfluous: we *pretend* to speak, as if on a theatrical stage. Nonetheless, something does occur in this otherwise pleonastic fiction. According to Husserl, "when someone says to himself 'You have gone wrong, you can't go on like that,'" we are not truly speaking, but we simply perform a rather strange action: "one merely conceives of oneself as speaking and communicating."[23] We know that this staging of the self as "speaking person" is neither parasitical nor extravagant (like Husserl seems to think), but rather constitutes an insuppressible, although mostly non-perceived, aspect of every enunciation. The crucial point is that the individual engaged in self-talk *isolates* and *showcases* this aspect of speech. In a well-articulated monologue we get used to representing the fact of speech, precisely because we have no communicative thrust. Freed from specific informational tasks, the signifying voice theatrically tells us about the linguistic faculty.

"You were wrong, you can't go on like this," "Stop it," "Come back," "Lord, have mercy": these expressions are absolute performatives, albeit implicit ones. Their ultimate meaning is "to say: 'I say.'" The passage from silent verbal thought to articulate monologue satisfies the need to "represent ourselves as speaking people." In other terms, they express the necessity to go back to the transcendental presupposition of any elocution (the linguistic faculty) through a specific empirical enunciation. This necessity, as we have already said, arises at certain critical junctures in our existence. In order to alleviate a malaise, sometimes we need to ritually retrace certain steps in anthropo- and ontogenesis. One of these steps is undoubtedly the child's egocentric language, which allows for the building of self-awareness and the individuation of the speaker.

11. Religious discourse

Only religious discourse is always powerful, pregnant with consequences, operational. From prayers to miracles, from blessings to confessions, from invocation to blasphemy, this discourse only communicates what it *does* while being enunciated. Even if it may seem telluric or monumental, the religious field shows in a particularly intense way the performativity and rituality of human language.

The study of linguistic acts, when undertaken with sober, scientific rigor (or rather, with materialistic intent), necessarily culminates in a theological inquiry.

However, the hypothesis that we want to develop does not focus on the general and complicated connection between liturgy and speech acts. It is, rather, a more vast and controversial thesis: religious language is first and foremost the privileged space of the absolute performative, that is, of the speech act that affirms to accomplish only and exclusively the act of speaking. Therefore, the logical form of religious enunciations is "I speak." Differently from ordinary performatives ("to swear," "to baptize," "to bet" and so on) ceremonial sentences are not limited to the mentioning of the reality created *by* speech, but also explicitly refer to the reality *of* speech. The distinctive markers of sacred discourse are the indeterminacy (or the stereotypical nature) weighing on the communicative message and the related prominence attributed to the enunciative act. We can think, for instance, about the liturgical value of repetition: the accumulation of identical and almost insignificant invocations, the triple enunciation that makes magical spells effective, the fact that "every cult is an eternal beginning."[24] Ritual reiteration distracts us from the dictum as specific propositional content, thereby encouraging the most strenuous attention for any further phonic incipit and the simple fact of speech. And this is only one of the many possible examples. Liturgical discourse, as legitimate representative of the absolute performative, keeps showing the *advent* of the Word in the world. If what is said each time illustrates *how* language works, the action of enunciating shows *that* language exists. Here we can perceive one (not the only but not the less significant one either) of the separations between the sacred and the profane: what we say is a sublunary matter, but the fact of speaking guarantees the exchange between man and God.

An analysis of religious language would demand a separate study and, most of all, a different author. What is at stake here are only those aspects of this speech that reveal the formal structure of the absolute performative. Let us start with some short remarks on *God as Word* and the *Word of God.*

In an admirable essay, Benveniste tells us that blasphemy is a pure speech process, since it consists in loudly transgressing the biblical interdiction of pronouncing the name of God: "We need to pay attention to the nature of an interdiction with is not based on 'saying something' as opinion, but on 'pronouncing a name,' that is, on a pure vocal articulation."[25] But why would the emission of a certain sound, a pure vocal articulation, have such shattering emotional implications? Where does the numinous power of the signifier "God" come from, a power respected by the pious and defied by the blasphemous? The fact is that "God" (as "this" or "I," by the way) is a word that only denotes the linguistic reality instituted by its own enunciation. Since the notion of "God" coincides with the act "to say: 'God,'" the act of saying the sacred name has to be expelled from free linguistic circulation, it has to be surrounded by precautions and made more precious by a systematic omission. Contrary to what might be supposed by some "materialists," the fact that there is no God outside of the name "God" does not diminish, but rather exalts religious fervor. At the beginning of the 20th century, the orthodox monks residing on Mount Athos deduced some rather extreme consequences from the disquieting coincidence between the word and the signified object. Their thesis overturns the biblical interdiction thanks to the reasons presented in its favor. If God is an eminently linguistic reality, only those who actively pronounce his name can experience his real presence. God, once again, is incarnated in a perceivable *flatus vocis*. In 1913, the Sacred Synod of the Orthodox Church condemned the nominalist enthusiasm of the monks as heretical, but the discussion continued with various results. The philosopher and mathematician Pavel Florensky was one of the defenders of the conviction held by the hermits living on Mount Athos: he argued that only in its clearly articulated name can we experience the deity's uninterrupted revelation. Emile Benveniste presents a concise, enlightening and probably involuntary version of this same controversial thesis when he writes: "We curse the name of God because this name is all we have of him. Only by invoking his name, whether to bless or to curse it, can we reach God."[26]

God is something *because* those who blandish or curse him speak and vocalize his name. What is sacred is not a specific referent, but the enunciating act. All opinions and dogmas on the nature of God (and therefore the possible semantic content of his name) stem from the incessant discourse—to use Benveniste's terms, the "formal apparatus of the enunciation"—that has been created by the religious tradition. Omnipotence, ubiquity, creation *ex nihilo*: these and all other divine attributes are the sublimated elaboration of certain traits characteristic of the enunciating act (but only when it is artificially separated from the text of the enunciation). The name "God" resumes and sanctifies a pervasive aspect of human speech: the fact of speaking which, just like God, is only made present by a phonic enunciation. Any word or enunciation, no matter how banal, shares the prerogatives proper to the sacred name every time their communicative message becomes indifferent and what is emphasized is the simple operation of the signifying voice. In other words: the name "God" is the venerable hypostasis of all linguistic usages resulting in an absolute performative. The "pure vocal articulation" founding both the pious invocation of the hermits and the ravings of the blasphemous is also the true goal of the enunciation "I speak." The absolute performative, by showing the linguistic faculty (or maybe, showing *that* language exists), transfers in innumerable secular utterances the highest virtues of the *nomen Dei*. Theologically speaking, it could be compared to the baptismal water or to the wine of the Eucharist: in conclusion, it resembles a sacrament.

The word of God anticipates our redemption; it is a good tiding, *evangelium*. But we should notice that it realizes what it announces, while and because it announces it. In his *Religion in Essence and Manifestation*, Gerardus van der Leeuw writes that the word of God "is the first place of the announcement, the message of salvation; but it is also this salvation itself, as it is revealed in the actual event."[27] The fact that God speaks, that he speaks to us, that he may break his silence to show himself to us is redemptive in itself. It doesn't matter if his sentences are enigmatic or even threatening: what really counts is that they are spoken. The simple enunciation of the divine word institutes a protective proximity between creature and creator. It goes without saying that the Word is the decisive proof of its unconditional performativity when, according to the Christian tradition, it becomes flesh and therefore breath and material sound. The audible signifying voice of the incarnated God neither explains nor describes: it realizes the presence of the Word in the World, a presence that is both the promise and the fulfillment of salvation.

Blessings and curses are a degraded and imperfect—but not dissimilar—version of certain traits of the word of God. When blessing or cursing, we use on an infinitesimal scale and split in two opposite practices the power inherent to the enunciating act that the Word (at least in Christianity) only proffers with a redemptive intent. Van Der Leeuw writes that "the curse is an effect of a power that requires no gods nor spirits to execute it."[28] He continues by saying that "the blessing, 'word-salvation' as it was called in the ancient German word [...] is by no means a mere pious wish, but the allocation of fortune's gifts by employing words."[29] Those who engage in these acts might dispense with the gods, precisely because they are reproducing on a limited scale the performativity typical of divine speech.

Like the name of God, also the verbs "to bless" and "to curse" have no reality outside their concrete enunciation. The meaning of these verbs (once again like "this" and "I") coincides with the enunciating act. But differently from "God" (and of "this" and "I"), "to bless" and "to curse" explicitly refer to the enunciation that realizes them: they both contain "–to say" as constitutive element. The presence of "–to say" distinguishes "to bless" and "to curse" also from delocutive verbs, which do designate the act of enunciating a sentence ("to salute" means "to say: '*salus*'") but don't mention at all the discursive activity that they are performing. With regard to the verb "to bless," Benveniste remarks: "precisely because the two components maintain their autonomy, *bene dicere* could not replace the true delocutive that would have been a verb directly derived from *bene*."[30] What is happening then?

The situation exemplified by *bene dicere* and *male dicere* is in a certain way similar to the absolute performative "I speak," whose adequate paraphrases is, as we know "to say: "I say." In those two verbs, the verb "dire" appears on both sides of the colon: "to bless" means "to say: 'I say (a good thing),'" while "to curse" means "to say: I say (a bad thing).'" They are also very compressed expressions, since the act of speaking, apart from being a logical constant ("to say: 'X'), is also a decisive part of the variable ('X': '*I say* (a good thing)’). It is true, of course, that differently from the simple “to say: ‘I say’” in this case we find in two opposite qualifications: we say either *good* or *bad* things. But, we might ask, how are the good and the bad things performed by blessings and curses defined? Certainly, they are not a benefit or a loss determined on the basis of a content, nor do they refer to a good or bad pronunciation. What those two verbs evoke is the “good” and the “evil” inherent to the speech act in itself. Through them, the act of enunciation affirms its own apotropaic or destructive power while realizing it. The religious formula “I bless you” and “I curse you” make completely visible the protection and the dangers of speech. In other words, they exemplify the ethical value of all absolute performatives.

12. Sacred languages

Religious practice is based on the tension—and the partial bifurcation—between the act and the contents of speech. It celebrates the distinction between speech and historic-natural languages. It regulates the hiatus between the generic power to speak and the set of possible or actual texts. Liturgical praxis can progressively fill this separation by reconciling the two poles that it institutes, or on the contrary it can radicalize this contrast and make it irrevocable (this later possibility prevails, obviously, in mystical experience).

The linguistic faculty, taken separately from the historic-natural languages, appears most of all as a *sui generis* “language”: the special idiom of all cults, an almost incomprehensible jargon, an eccentric dialect exclusively employed at the borders between human and eternal worlds. The linguistic faculty, although more universal than any single natural language, is present in a paradoxically restricted area of speech. In its stead, we find artificial and marginal forms of speech, quite external to ordinary use. Think, for instance, about the openly meaningless—or at least obscure—nature of certain ceremonial words, such as *alleluia*, *kyrie eleison*, *amen*, *om om*: according to Van Der Leeuw, "a mystical tone-colour is attached to them; while their very incomprehensibility enhances their numinous power. Frequently, a special cult language thus arises."[31]

In addition to a vocabulary without (or with very little) semantic consistency, religious rituals rely on many other expedients to distance themselves from the historic-natural language of their own community. Very often, they adopt *dead languages*. We will only mention some important examples: the adoption of the archaic Avestan alphabet in Iranian liturgy, the recourse to Sanskrit in Chinese and Japanese sacred Buddhist ceremonies, the use of classical Hebrew among Aramaic-speaking worshippers, and the persistence of Latin in Catholic ritual before the Second Vatican Council. In the most ancient religions, sometimes writing itself performed the function of ritual idiolect, as a pseudo-language able to guarantee the communication with the gods. In general, dead languages (like foreign or written ones) conjure in a sensory way all that goes beyond the institutional field of each and every language: it materializes in specific but unfamiliar sounds the common and indeterminate linguistic faculty. Similar to the child immersed in a solitary monologue, the faithful repeating "Om" or "Amen," or reciting psalms in an otherwise unknown and obsolete language, distances him or herself from the maternal tongue and inhabits the no-man's land of linguistic competence, which is the biological-potential characteristic of the species.

Glossolalia—the compulsive invention of meaningless words —is undoubtedly the prototype for any ritual language. Documented in primitive Christianity and in many ancient and modern religious movements, it represents an intermediate stage between linguistic faculty and natural languages, an ambivalent threshold between the two, the abyss often gaping under the translator's feet. Van der Leeuw writes that "the person who expresses his emotions in glossolalia speaks without desiring to do so; in many instances he appears to feel himself impleaded to speak, in others perhaps even this is not the case ; he speaks like a machine, or more precisely, something speaks through him. He knows not the content of what he says in advance, but interprets his words and understands them afterwards, as if they were those of another person."[32] Very similar to glossolalia are religious chants. The anthropologist Clarisse Herrenschmidt says the following:

> The Guayaki warriors around the fire by night, huddled together [...] Each warrior sings a recitative producing such a cacophony that no one could hear or understand anything. It is one and the same harsh speech of glorification of himself [...]: "I," "I," "I." Sung in the presence of others, this speech was, however, solitary, uttered to the void. Here, too, language was not of the men and the speech was not of the subject.[33]

Glossolalia, a pure non-language or a radically foreign idiom, expresses the extreme but significant penitential humility that is the hallmark both of the religious rituals staged by the faithful and the production of an absolute performative by a miscreant speaker. In both cases, when we want to return to the generic power and abandon our maternal language, we need to cross the narrow entry represented by the decomposition of the semantic content. In both cases, we heed the evangelic admonition to lower ourselves so that we may be exalted: only those who are indifferent or even derisive toward their own communicative message can represent themselves as bearers of the linguistic faculty.

No matter the specific aspects (obsolete language, glossolalia and so on) that it assumes, according to Van Der Leeuw ritual language always boils down to a particular form of *silence*: "The standard terminology of liturgy, no detail of which can be arbitrarily changed and which is employed with the utmost conservatism, is itself an approximation to silence."[34] We should be careful though: what is silenced is the speaker, as author of a specific *dictum* or of a message. The mechanical utterance of a sacred text drowns all other sounds. The ritual "silence" is the obliteration of what is said. In this case, the speaker is the one who's truly silent (for instance, reciting a prayer in a foreign language). Therefore, the speaker reduces his or her locutory performance to the mere emission of articulated sounds. Florensky says:

> A healer muttering formulas whose meaning is unknown even to her, or a priest reciting prayers that are in part incomprehensible to him, are not as absurd a figure as it might seem at first glance. As soon as the formula is pronounced, its intention is clearly indicated and specified: it is the intention of uttering the formula.[35]

The semantic silence constituting the horizon of religious rituals is very noisy. Far from excluding phonic enunciations, it requires and profits from them. It is a silence "for voice only": it is demanded and sustained by a voice that is *only voice*.

When it is ritually removed from historic-natural languages, the linguistic faculty partially coagulates in pure sound, coinciding with the activity of the phonatory organs. In ritual, vocalization is obsessively regulated, precisely because it symbolizes the linguistic faculty.

The butchering or the omission of a sacred text by a believer can have fatal consequences. This is what Van Der Leeuw says about the operational power (that is, the performativity) of phonology in a religious context: "Those who speak unleash certain powers. The power of the words increases in various ways. Speaking louder, emphasizing or insisting on certain formula, combining rhythm and rhyme: these are all elements conferring a greater energy to speech."[36] And he adds: "Whoever can pronounce accurately his script and has 'the right voice' can confront the world's dangers."[37] As we read in Aeschylus' *Coëphores*, we need to "show the power of the mouth." This power adopts the most different registers: the voice exerts a ritual function not only by assuming decisive and thundering tones, but also adapting to a "pianissimo," to an exhausted whispering. The oscillations typical of religious speech can go to the point of stuttering: this is the sign of the fearful hesitancy that should always surround the enunciating act and its inherently ritual nature.

The emission of sounds, the movement of the tongue against the palate, the modification of the air flow are the indispensable logical conditions of the absolute performative (since, as we know, they guarantee the integral self-referentiality of "I speak") and also valuable *ritual* elements of religious practice. The centrality of phonation in the liturgical context shows to what extent religious experience is tied to the physiological aspects of human language. Only the signifying voice, and not any particular message, can act as a medium between the speaker and his or her God. Only the voice allows the single speaker to access an immense biological (phylo- and ontogenetic) heritage that, transcending any specific enunciation, always retains a divine character. Only an unequivocal recognition of the role performed by phonation in religious praxis allows us to understand in a more adequate—that is, less condescending and high-handed—way what was meant by Ludwig Feuerbach, an author that has been mistreated by continental and analytic philosophers alike: "God is the idea of the species as an individual."[38] And indeed, the individual speaker experiences his or her unity with the species through the emission of articulated sounds. This is why this emission is what really counts and endures when we address God verbally (since God is the concept of this unity). And this is why the voice is *sacred.*

The tension between linguistic faculty and natural languages culminates in the confession. The contrast between communicative message and the simple enunciating act is never as touching and dramatic as in this ritual. The absolute performative never acquires a more delicate role. The sinner who confesses to an evil action, such as a violent robbery or even a homicide, expresses a terrible semantic content, no matter the language used, be it Italian, Portuguese or anything else. To expiate such a crime, however, he or she can't but talk about it. In this case, the enunciating act constitutes the only effective antidote against the poison contained in the text of the enunciations. Speech, by transcending the borders of the single languages and reasserting the linguistic faculty, *un-says* the evil it describes, and thereby alleviates and heals it. What we say during confession is, quite literally, the evil that we need to expiate; only the fact of speaking is *redemptive.*

13. On praying

Prayers, which are so important in religious rituals, extend and develop the child's egocentric language, inheriting some of its essential functions and unabashedly adopting its modalities, although with infinite complications: the adoring or imploring crowd of the faithful emits a series of "collective monologues" where echolalia, fabulation and annunciations prevail.

We have already seen that infantile egocentric language, contrary to Vygotsky's assertions, doesn't fully evolve into adult, silent verbal thought. Many of its crucial characteristics—precisely those that determine the development of self-awareness and the principle of individuation—are indissolubly tied to vocalization. Instead, the stigmata of audible infantile soliloquy resurface in the actual words of the experienced and astute speaker who simply affirms "I speak." They resurface in the language games characterized by the production of absolute performatives. The best examples for this behavior are the external monologues used by the adult to encourage or admonish him or herself: "You were wrong, you can't go on like this," "Stop it," "Lord have mercy" and so on. But these are the very phonic outbursts that break the silence of verbal thought, and that can be rightfully compared to religious prayers.

The clearest resemblance between the prayer pronounced in a church and the monologue of a troubled adult is their shared *superfluity*. Let's remember Husserl's observation: since the speaker, when talking to him or herself, does not communicate "the existence of mental experiences" that are already perfectly known, monologues are expressions without content, completely useless from an informational point of view. Prayers are equally pleonastic, since also in their case it might seem that we are only *pretending* to speak. Just as the solitary speaker has no need to be informed about his or her own "mental experiences," so the worshipper doesn't need to tell God about his or her thoughts and wishes, since God is already aware of them. In the treaty *De Magistro*, Saint Augustin reflects on the redundancy of vocalized prayer: "Augustin—Then doesn't it seem to you that speaking is undertaken only for the sake of teaching or reminding? Adeodatus: It would seem so were I not troubled by the fact that we certainly speak while we're praying, and yet it isn't right to believe that we teach God or remind Him of anything."[39] Shortly thereafter, Augustin explains that prayers, with their dearth of informational messages, are not pronounced so that God, but that men may listen, "and by remembering might, with one accord, be raised to God."[40] The two interlocutors finally agree that "in the case of praying to God, Who we cannot suppose is taught or reminded, words are for the purpose either of reminding ourselves or that others may be reminded or taught by us."[41] Otherwise superfluous prayers still need to be said so that *we may represent ourselves as speaking*. Internal exhortation and proximity to God hinge on this self-reflective representation. The pious speaker is comforted and purified by this self-staging as source of enunciations and support for the signifying voice. Also according to Husserl, "the expressions of solitary life" consist simply in presenting oneself as a person capable of speech. Both those who say to themselves: "You were wrong, you can't go on like this" and those who implore: "Lord, forgive me" are simply staging their linguistic faculty, they prove that they *can* speak. In truth, they are one and the same linguistic form. Religious prayers strengthen and regulate the vocalized soliloquies of the adult, conferring on them a ritual appearance. But since these monologues perpetuate many of the peculiar characteristics of the child's egocentric language, we can also say that prayers are an *egocentric language in the second degree*.

Representing oneself as speaker—prayer's most important task and benefit—is also the foundation of the principle of individuation. The child distances him or herself from pre-individual life by appearing as the singular bearer of the linguistic faculty that is the substratum of the biological power to speak. Prayer renews that distance. It can either valorize or reinstate the speaker's individuation. However, it is clear that the necessity to emphasize or to reaffirm this individuation is only felt in times of *crisis*. Religious prayers perfectly document the periodical crises traversed by individuation, while at the same time they constitute an effective way to face and overcome them. By enunciating superfluous words that communicate nothing, we signal the effacement of the speaker's singularity but we also help in restoring it. As sign of the erasure of individuation, prayer is *an inverted ontogenesis*, that is, a return to the pre-individual reality that we partially left during our childhood. On the other hand, as remedy to the crisis and reassertion of our individuation, prayer is *a ritually duplicated ontogenesis*.

We pray with abandonment (or, in a more pedestrian way, we burst into self-directed exclamations such as "You can't go on like this") when we are threatened in our singularity. For a moment, the pressure of pre-individual life seems unsustainable. The well-differentiated "I" is no longer an unquestionable certainty: on the contrary, we have the impression that it is dissipating in an indefinite world.

Prayer manifests an ambiguous situation, where there is a more or less complete fusion between the individual and the species, that is, between the "I" and "God." Eugène Minkowski writes: "It is wrong to say that when we pray there are a God and an I addressing him; this is already an analysis of the phenomenon that we want to study."[42] What is primordial and inevitable is the slippery unity of the two poles, the indistinction between addresser and addressee. Paul Tillich comments on the strange and even jarring fact that we speak "to somebody to whom [we] cannot speak, because he is not 'somebody' [...] saying 'Thou' to somebody who is closer to the 'I' than the 'I' is to itself."[43] In a way, the invoked God is the opposite of individuality (he is not 'somebody'), but he is also so close to us that he's what is most familiar to us ("closer to the I than the I is to itself"). When we pray, we are awed by the *intimacy* of pre-individuality, that is, the prevalence of the biological traits of the species right into the remotest parts of our psyche. There is also an extreme case. When we understand the fragility of the I, we can also decide to abandon all doubt and to radicalize the crisis of individuation. In that case, we have a decisive conversion to an impersonal existence: rather than fearing it, we desire it and are grateful for it. Simone Weil, who staunchly pursued this existence, writes: "We possess nothing in the world—a mere chance can strip us of everything—except the power to say I. That is what we have to give to God—in other words, to destroy."[44] And she adds: "Once we have understood we are nothing, the object of all our efforts is to become nothing [...] it is for this that we pray. May God grant me to become nothing."[45] For Weil, the deity comes into contact with the human being only if the latter stops being human; only if, through prayer, the human being disposes of its cumbersome singularity.

So, even if religious prayers (just like egocentric language) are a form of self-directed speech, we still have to add that this "self" acquires unstable and fragile traits.

Generally, when we feel that our individual life is flowing back to the indifferentiation of pre-individuality, we try—unless we share Simone Weil's inclinations—to reactivate the principle of individuation. This is why we have recourse to prayer, an egocentric language of the second degree, even if it shows the fragility and the gaps of individuation. Obviously, this apotropaic reaction does not express the distinctive traits of a specific I: what is now in danger and needs to be preserved is precisely the I as unitary substratum for well-connected and unique memories and biographical notes.

Prayer is not an *individual* action, since its task is the ritual emancipation of the speaker through an impersonal experience. It is, rather, an *individuating* act. It recapitulates and renews the passage from the anonymous "we" to the "I." Glossolalia, which is a particularly fervent form of prayer, perfectly exemplifies this remark: nothing is less individual of a sequence of meaningless sounds, but at the same time nothing is more individuating than the simple act of speaking, which allows the faithful to demonstrate the inherence of the generic power to speak to his particular living body. And indeed, all enunciations whose ultimate meaning is "I speak" are not individual, but individuating.

Prayer, precisely because it is pleonastic from the point of view of communication (God already knows what we tell him), allows the speaker to represent him or herself as bearer of the linguistic faculty, as contingent and unique personification of the biological ability to speak. In ritual prayer we witness anew—after having experienced its temporary decline—the incarnation of the Word in a mortal body. The eminently naturalistic core of the individuating principle is concentrated in the most enigmatic verse of John's Gospel: *Et verbum caro factum est.*

14. *In limine*

Let's conclude. The absolute performative "I speak" is the logic form, or at least the most adequate paraphrasis, of all language games that emphasize the fact of speech in itself, while their specific communicative message becomes secondary or negligible. In our first seven sections, we studied the structure and forms of the absolute performative (its relation with the enunciatory acts and the delocutive verbs, the primacy of vocalization, the immunity from the threat of inefficacy or vacuity and so on). We then explored two specific fields where the enunciation "I speak" plays a crucial role: infantile egocentric language and religious speech.

The absolute performative is situated at the crossing of important philosophical issues. The most important ones, all interconnected and even juxtaposed, are: a) the distinction between linguistic faculty and historic-natural languages; b) the processes leading to self-awareness; c) the principle of individuation; d) the linguistic foundation of the rituality typical of the human animal; e) the periodic need to recapitulate the essential steps of anthropogenesis for apotropaic purposes. The most important thing is the empirical, factual aspect taken by these issues when we analyze in the light of the absolute performative. The language games that privilege the enunciating act, making the content of the enunciation almost irrelevant, confer a full and immediate visibility to the transcendental presuppositions of communication. The conditions of possibility for our experience are also among the facts that we actually live through. The hidden foundations of human speech appear as a peculiar discursive phenomenon; in other words, they appear as a specific *way of saying*. The absolute performative, therefore, is the instrument of a materialistic kind of revelation that allows the root to emerge from the ground; or rather, to show that it was always there.

The linguistic games dominated by the enunciation "I speak" appear in the most different contexts, and at their limits. They intervene when a certain way of life is no longer taken for granted, and becomes difficult and controversial. The use of the absolute performative signals the "state of emergency" incurred by an experience that until then had been a safe context for a certain praxis.

Now that we are nearing the end, we might still want to formulate a further hypothesis, nothing more than a remark, a promise to be kept later. Here it is: in contemporary forms of life the absolute performative is no longer marginal, or interstitial, but occupies the center of the stage; no longer is it the signal of a "state of emergency," but presides to our daily business. The language games based on the enunciation "I speak" (that is, on the very manifestation of the linguistic faculty) are today at the very core of social communication. We can think about how our organization of labor relies on the generic (potential, biological) linguistic competency of the human animal: in the execution of innumerable tasks and functions what matters is not the familiarity with a certain kind of enunciations, but the ability to produce any sort of enunciations; it doesn't matter what we say, but the simple ability to say it.

This thesis entails at least one, very important consequence. We have already said that the absolute performative affords us the opportunity to recapitulate certain steps of anthropogenesis. We have also said that we make use of this opportunity when faced with certain difficulties and crises. But this is only true as long as the absolute performative remains a marginal instrument operating *at the limits* of every form of life, without constituting the essence of any of them. Things change, of course, when it becomes the foundation of our daily linguistic practice. If it is true that the enunciation "I speak" is the hallmark of today's communications society, then we should recognize that the repetition of anthropogenesis is no longer an apotropaic resource to be used in times of crisis, but an immediate and quite considerable *content of ordinary experience.* In other words, we would need to say that human praxis has arrived to the point of pondering and experiencing its own preconditions, that it has enrolled as raw material the differential traits of the species, and that it is invested in the most direct way with the elements constituting human praxis.

3

The Repetition of Anthropogenesis

1. De Martino: the making and unmaking of self-consciousness

Ernesto De Martino argued that anthropogenesis is an unstable and to a certain extent reversible end result. The essential traits of the human animal are not a permanently acquired ground facing the tumultuous vicissitudes and the occasional defeats of historical praxis. The risk of collapse or recession sometimes concerns precisely those basic prerogatives. The ground as such is questioned, becoming the epicenter of a crisis.

In the first place, De Martino examines the making and unmaking of self-consciousness. Far from being an unconditioned presupposition, as Kant thought, the "synthetic unit of apperception" is the uncertain outcome of a historic-natural journey. We never fully complete it, so much so that often we retrace it backwards. In a crucial passage of *Primitive Magic*, a book that had the privilege of attracting the ire and mockery of all the different idealist schools of Italian philosophy, De Martino writes:

> Besides this, the supreme principle of the transcendental unity of self-awareness involves a supreme risk to the person—the risk, or threat of losing the supreme principle through which it is constituted

> and established. This risk appears when the person, instead of retaining his autonomy in his relationship to the contents, abdicates, and allows the contents to act, outside of the synthesis, is as undominated elements, as 'given facts' in the absolute sense. When confronted with this threat, it is the person itself that is in danger of disintegrating, of disappearing as presence [...]. Kant adopted the analytical unit of apperception as a non-historical and uniform given fact—that is, the thought that belongs to the self, and does not change with its contents, but considers them as an integral part; and then placed the transcendental condition of this given fact within the synthetic unit of apperception. But elements and given facts of the consciousness do not exist (except through abstraction), nor does a presence exist—there is no empirical being-within-the-world that is a given fact, an original immediate that is sheltered from all danger and incapable, within its own sphere, of any dram or development, or any *history*.[1]

The "I think" is not a guaranteed process: in certain situations it can even become the prize to be gained. Instead of delving into the different strategies employed by our consciousness to metabolize a loss or a failure, De Martino explores the failures and the losses incurred by consciousness itself, which are impossible to metabolize. The *Bildungsroman* of the human animal constantly rewrites its first chapter, where the distinctive traits of the species are yet to become fully visible and the transcendental categories openly show the traces of their empirical origins.

De Martino also analyzes the doing and undoing of what Heidegger called our being-in-the-World. An early (but far from servile) reader of *Being and Time*, he believes that the fundamental relation I/World is also vulnerable to the risk of a radical dissolution. Also in this case, De Martino does not focus on the negative possibilities of a certain modality of human existence, but on its possible obsolescence. For him, what counts are not the anxiety or the boredom that we might feel in the world, but the eclipse of all worldly experience, anxiety and boredom included. The study of psychopathology and the history of religions both illustrate with exemplary clarity the fragility of the anthropogenetic process. According to De Martino, the eschatological myth of the end of the world emphasizes the risk of "not-being-there-in-any-possible-world."[2] This is not the arbitrary product of theological speculations, or simply a cultural rough spot: it is the symptom manifesting a natural property of our species. The belief in the periodical destructions and regenerations of the cosmos ("one of the philogenetically most ancient human attitudes"[3]) is tied to the biological configuration of the most evolved of primates who, lacking specialized instincts, has to deal with a partially undetermined vital context (*the world*) and not a largely predictable *environment*. The Last Day is always on the program: in the way of being of the human animal what is contingent are not only certain specific experiences, but the very conditions of experience, at least to a certain degree.

Crisis and reversibility of the synthetic unit of apperception, crisis and reversibility of our being-in-the-world: if we radicalize just a bit the diagnosis proposed by De Martino, we could say that human nature is characterized by its eternal preoccupation with the origin of man as separate species. In other words, the distinctive character of the *anthropos* is *the constant repetition of anthropogenesis*. The inaugural act does not disappear in a fully archived "previous otherness," but remains in the foreground and is contemporary of all the concrete articulations of our social and political praxis. Our prehistory is inscribed in every single historical moment.

2. Saussure: the origin as permanent condition

Everyone knows that *Homo sapiens* has existed for about 100,000 years. How can we say, then, that its origins are still visible? Obviously, we don't struggle every morning to stand erect. There are, of course, evolutionary processes that we cannot remember and that are not reproduced in any of our daily experiences. Human tactility presupposes, and does not repeat, the liberation of the hand from the task of perambulation. There has to be a limiting criterion: the genesis of a species can still be considered a present phenomenon only for those aspects that fully coincide with the ordinary functioning of that particular species. Anthropogenesis is visible and recurrent when constitutive processes and fully developed schemes, beginning and routine, *natura naturans* and *natura naturata* are mostly indiscernible. Of all the processes where the result faithfully executes the promise and humanization is concomitant with human nature, the most important is verbal language.

According to the scholars of cognition, there is a missed, or rather impossible, link between Saussure and the theories on the evolution of the species. Too bad for Saussure, they seem to imply. He was only concerned with language as complete and coherent system, lightheartedly neglecting the birth records of human speech, the umbilical cord connecting it to previous forms of thought and communication. This is an insidious but rather unfounded critique. If we look closely, structural linguistics suggested the methodological principle most capable of shedding light on the iterative character of anthropogenesis. Saussure does not avoid the question of the origin of language. On the contrary, he expands it to the point of making it coincide with the study of every enunciation. He writes: "in dealing with speech, it is completely misleading to assume that the problem of early characteristic differs from the problem of permanent characteristics."[4]

Let us consider these words very carefully: do they really mean that language is born fully formed? You can believe it if you want; being prejudiced is not a crime. I believe the contrary to be true: for Saussure, language always brings with itself, even in its most complex and ancient manifestations, the weaknesses and impurities of its origins. It is useless to look for an original state of language, precisely because it never left such a state. It makes no sense to go back to an *incipit*, since we are still nailed to it. The origins are always upon us, like an unpaid bill. Descriptive linguistics, if it accomplishes its task scrupulously, inevitably delineates a *logo-genesis*. What was at the beginning endures untouched in the experience of every speaker. The current functioning of our conversations incessantly repeats the "primal scene" of human elocutions. The linguistic animal is, in other words, a *semel*-born one.

According to this interpretation of Saussure's words, the question we should ask is the following: which aspects of the "permanent conditions" are mirrored by their "origins"? And vice versa: what, in those "origins," is never fully resolved but instead becomes a rule and an ordinary occurrence? I will limit myself to a conceptually rather simple remark, since a more adequate analysis of this issue is to be found later. Human verbal language has a negative foundation: it arises from the lack of a sign code biunivocally tied to the different configurations of the surrounding environment. This lack, together with the generic physiological ability to emit articulated sounds, defines most pertinently what we call the linguistic *faculty*. Faculty means potentiality. Potential is what has no autonomous importance, but rather bears the marks of in-actuality and latency. Only the animal that is born aphasic possesses the linguistic faculty.

The logogenetic passage goes from potentiality to actuality, from undefined faculty to specific speech, from initial aphasia to contingent verbal executions. This is a chronic, or rather *recursive* passage: it did not happen once for all, during the age of the Cro- Magnon or in our infancy, but it characterizes the entire experience of the speaker. Emile Benveniste fully grasps the iterative nature of anthropogenesis, for instance when he observes that all speakers, when they form a sentence, need to "appropriate the language."[5] The necessity of appropriation indicates a previous state of lack and aphasia that we need to overcome every time we speak. The anthropogenetic stage has not been definitely abandoned *illo tempore*: this stage constitutes as such the permanent territory of the linguistic animal. The "once upon a time" becomes similar to the "once more."

Let's take the communication code of the bees, Aesop's analogy that has long figured in the philosophy of language. The dances that allow these hymenoptera to signal the direction and the distance separating them from the place where there is food simply execute a score already specified in all of its parts. The essential traits of this score-code are "the fixity of its subject matter, the invariability of the message, the relation to a single set of circumstances, the impossibility of separating the components of the message, and its unilateral transmission."[6] In fact, the score of the bees has a filogenetic origin that is not extended to its current operations and neither is it repeated by them: the communicative message expressed by the circular movement of the honey bee presupposes a code but does not restage its constitution. Human language, instead, consists in the lack of any definite score and in the potential to create all sort of scores, as a "restricted number of morphemes, or elements of meaning, can be reduced to even less numerous 'phonemes,' or elements of articulation, devoid of meaning.

[...] It is the selective and distinctive grouping of these elements of articulation which produces meaning."[7] The recurrent passage from potentiality to action—or also, in another way, from phoneme to morpheme—correspond to what was for the bees the filogenetic creation of the score-code. Precisely because it is an amorphous and inchoate potentiality, the linguistic faculty is not an independent presupposition, endowed with its own positive reality. Although it seems paradoxical, this faculty only appears in its executions, inseparable from them as the shadow from the body. In turn, its conditions of possibility are supported by the phenomena that this faculty makes possible. The passage from faculty to execution doesn't take logogenesis for granted; rather, it is its exact copy. When we break the silence and start to speak, we reproduce on a small scale the primal scene of human discourse, since "before the enunciation the language is only the possibility of language." The couple potentiality/action always plays a double game: it is a beginning and ordinary administration, "once upon a time" and "once more."[8]

This is true not only of verbal language, but of human temporality in general. Also in this case we can speak of a full coincidence between origins and permanent conditions. And even more importantly, in the case of chronogenesis this coincidence is also reducible to the couple potentiality/action. We can easily understand that there is no trace of time if we don't have the experience of the *not-now*. The essential condition of becoming is a lack of contemporaneity, a whole in the net of the *now*. The eternal present of God, or of the animal caught in its environment, is not even a present: it actually constitutes an a-temporal way of being. When we say, "not now," we say potentiality. Potentials are absent by definitions, they have no independent reality, they are external to the course of time. When we say "now," we say actuality. Being in action means being present. Potentiality and actuality are temporal concepts. In fact, they are *temporalizing* concepts.[9] Their relation as heterogeneous parts is chronogenetic. The action temporarily puts in reserve the indeterminate potentiality; it escapes it for a moment. And that moment is "now." The only pertinent definition of "now," therefore, is "*no longer-not-now.*" Chronogenesis, that is the couple inactuality/presence, is at work in every fragment of becoming. All historical moments are made of potentiality and actions, of not-now and now, of an empty and a saturated aspect. All historical moments extend and renew the *incipit* of time. Also in this case, as for verbal enunciation, we constantly witness the small scale reproduction of an anthropogenetic episode. This is not a simple analogy: from a temporal point of view, what is the faculty of language if not a not-now, a persistent inactuality, a non-presence? And what is a speech-act, if not a now, that is a "no longer not-now"? Paraphrasing Saussure, we can say that when temporality is concerned it is completely wrong to believe that the problem of the origins is different from that of its permanent conditions.

At this point, we need to introduce some conceptual details. De Martino talks about a crisis of the anthropogenesis, or rather of its partial recession. But this crisis is only conceivable if anthropogenesis is always occurring. Only a current process can move backwards or fail, not an acquired result. Therefore, the basic condition of the crisis is the *semel*-born character of the human animal or, in other words, the coincidence between *incipit* and ordinary administration. Saussure postulated this coincidence with respect to language. However, this is also true for temporality in general, and we can reasonably hypothesize that this is also the case for self-consciousness and our being-in-the-world. If the crisis of anthropogenesis presupposes the latter's persistence and experiential nature, it also imposes—as a counter-poison—the reaffirmation of certain species-specific prerogatives of *the Homo sapiens*. In other words, it imposes the repetition of anthropogenesis. From now on, "repetition" will no longer mean a general recursive occurrence, but specifically the overcoming of a crisis. The identity of "origins" and "permanent conditions" postulated by Saussure is the ontological premise founding the two polarities studied by De Martino, that is, the apocalyptic collapse and the salvific reinstatement of the essential conditions of human praxis. This is the premise for our analysis of the forms taken by the crisis and of the modes of its overcoming.

3. The arrow and the cycle

Speech acts are contingent and unique. Their succession is unidirectional, conforming to the image of time as an irreversible *arrow*. But on the other hand, each of these acts is tied to the linguistic faculty, which has remained unchanged since the age of Cro-Magnon. All enunciations, no matter their particular content, always spring forth from the same potential for speech. The relation potentiality/action, therefore, follows a *cycle* bound to repeat itself. The arrow and the cycle are indirectly visible already in the single enunciation, if we distinguish its two concurrent but heterogeneous aspects: what is cyclical is the decision to speak, the breaking of the silence, the transition from potentiality to action; what is irreversible is the particular semantic content, the communicative message articulated here and now, in short, what we say in each instance. It goes without saying that the recurrent side of every verbal elocution (that is, the simple demonstration that we are able to speak) can also assume a contingent aspect if it becomes part of a single speech act. Inversely, if we want to stress the cyclical nature of the passage from faculty to execution in multiple enunciations, the specific content of the latter will become less important, becoming a simple variable dependent from the recursive nature of the decision to speak.

The relation potentiality/actuality is anthropogenetic. Its cyclical nature proves that any single molecule of our experience—although unrepeatable like all that happens in the arrow of time—reproduces on an infinitesimal scale the origin of the species. The cycle composed by the repetitions of anthropogenesis, far from inhibiting or paralyzing history, guarantees the mutability and irreparable contingency of the arrow. If instead of an inarticulate potentiality the linguistic faculty were a score-code, the origin would not be a permanent condition. But if this was true, there would not be a history marked by unforeseen events and full of swerves and variations. The arrow depends on the cycle. The praxis of the linguistic animal does not have a definite script, nor does it produce a final outcome, precisely because it continuously retraces anthropogenesis. The monotonous cyclical movements that re-actualize the uncertainty and disorientation inherent to the formative process of the species guarantee and encourage the proliferation of unprecedented and therefore surprising experiences.

We do, however, need to add a very important corollary to these theses: the relation potentiality/actuality is itself *potential.* This is why it can become fragile and even disintegrate. If it weren't so, if this relation knew no failure, it would not be a true (that is, indeterminate) potentiality, but only a detailed catalogue of possible executions. The cycle potentiality/actuality—which is both an origin and a permanent condition—can break down and even explode. Sometimes, the potentiality folds back on itself, without expressing itself in definite actions. Inversely, it can also happen that the action loses any potential character, acquiring the hallucinated fixity of the tic, or of the Pavlovian reflex. According to De Martino, these are in fact the two forms that manifest a crisis in the process of anthropogenesis.

The undoing of self-consciousness and of our being-in-the-world reach their crisis in the "loss of presence" (a term that De Martino employs intentionally, echoing the Heideggerian *Dasein*). The loss of presence, that is, of the *Dasein*, can have opposite and symmetric outcomes. It can either consist in a painful "lack of semanticity" or in an uncontrollable, inflationary whirlwind caused by "an excess of semanticity that cannot find a resolution in a definite meaning."[10] *The lack of semanticity* results in the reduction of human discourse to a limited series of monochord signals. The enunciations seem disconnected from the linguistic faculty, no longer subject to the variability that it implies. The I contracts in a series of stereotyped behaviors: what prevails is the forced repetition of the same formulas and gestures. The world dries out and is simplified to the point of resembling a theatrical backdrop. *The excess of semanticity*, instead, brings about the solitary dominance of the linguistic faculty: this is an inarticulate ability that can no longer become a univocal discourse. In this case, the I am reabsorbed in an amorphous, chaotic, purely potential universe. The objects are no longer discrete units, but they meld in an unstable and overwhelming *continuum*. The lack and the excess of semanticity instigate opposite fears: our bodily experience "becomes a barrier that is too rigid and separates us from the world without possibility of meaningful communication, or too fragile, traversed by the world in a chaotic manner."[11]

Acts without potential or, inversely, a potential without acts: in both cases, the anthropogenetic process is fissured and starts to regress. Ultimately, what is compromised is the nexus between repetition and irreversibility typical of human experience. And now let us consider the enunciations alone, disconnected from the linguistic faculty. At first sight, they still seem to follow the arrow of time. But this is not so. Once the cycle potentiality/actuality is broken, the arrow itself disappears: the enunciations/signals are stereotyped, rigid and predictable, never really contingent. They fall back into an "eternal present" of sorts. If we examine the opposite case, when the faculty of language struggles to perform adequate verbal executions, we see that we can no longer talk about repetitions: the persistence of a potentiality that is not accompanied by specific acts (by a "not-now" deprived of a "now") is no longer a cycle, rather resembling an unending paralysis. The arrow and the cycle fail together: "The excess or the lack of semanticity endangering the entire field of our possible worldly perceptions, the excess or the lack of distance of the world from our presence, or of our presence from the world [...] are strictly tied to a syndrome characterized by the refusal to change and act."[12]

4. Cultural apocalypses

A loss of presence needs its reconstitution necessary. The "no longer" that swallowed our self-awareness and our being-in-the-world has to become a "not yet"; recessive manifestations need to become precursory. In other words, we need to restore the preconditions of our experience, starting from the fundamental relation between potentiality and actuality sundered by the crisis.

De Martino believes that the repetition of anthropogenesis stems from a bizarre categorical imperative: our being-in-the-world, which per se is fragile and subject to catastrophe, is supported by an inescapable and fundamental "*having* to be there." Our chronically unstable Dasein is once again protected and reaffirmed thanks to an ethical impulse that considers presence a "value":

> That the *Dasein* is an *in-der-Welt-sein* is the fundamental theme of Heideggerian existentialism. But the *being-there* as *being-in-the-world* sends us back to the real transcendental condition of the *having* to be there. We can explain presence only as the deployment of the energy that creates the presence, as the values created by the emergence of life's immediacy: this means that this energy, this "beyond," constitutes the real transcendental condition of existence. The worldliness of being there refers to the having to be there [...] the human being is always implied in the need to transcend and in its different modalities. Only through this valorizing going beyond does human existence constitute itself, becomes a presence in the world, takes care of situations and duties and founds, modifies and takes part in the cultural order.[13]

I think that De Martino enters an impasse, or even worse: in his recourse to an "ethos of transcendence" (that is, to a *having* to be there), he accepts to live below his means, misjudging his own original premises. If we attribute the merit of renewing the process of becoming human to a categorical imperative, we no longer understand why this process had suffered a crisis or a regression. Was the "ethos of transcendence" dormant? That might be true, but then we have to explain why this can or cannot happen. The instability of self-consciousness and of the being-in-the-world fatally affects the categorical imperative itself. The problem is simply moved backwards, as if from a room to another: the supposed explanation still needs to be explained.

De Martino understood with enviable assurance the conditioned, and therefore precarious, nature of the "I think" and of the *Dasein*, of self-consciousness and the being-in-the-world. I repeat what I already said at the beginning: he didn't simply enumerate the various weaknesses of these fundamental characters of human nature, but he highlighted their possible disappearance as such. According to him, the most solid *a priori* is reversible: what can shift is not only the game table, but the prize at stake. The *a priori* can even be considered an *a posteriori*, since it can be either dismantled or reconstituted by the human praxis that makes it possible. The radicalism of this position is ill-suited to moralistic shortcuts. The ruin and the reconstitution of certain characteristics of the Homo sapiens cannot rest on the good health of an "ethos of transcendence." As it often happens, the invocation of a having to be there betrays—in the double sense of involuntarily revealing and distorting—the real question, which concerns *being* as such. The repetition of anthropogenesis is an ontological, not an ethical question. It addresses the biological constitution of our species, and not various cultural attitudes. The repetition, just as the crisis that it wants to confront, is rooted in the identity of "origins" and "permanent conditions" clearly stated by Saussure. This identity characterizes the whole mode of being of the linguistic animal. It is precisely because its genesis always remains in the foreground that the Homo sapiens is always involved in the process of becoming human, experiencing both its fragility and its constant reaffirmation. The origin, which is also an everyday occurrence, consists in the nexus between potentiality and actuality. But this nexus is also potential. It can exist, but it can also be missing. The loss of presence and its periodical reinstatement correspond to the loosening and the reconstitution of the couple potentiality/actuality.

De Martino calls a "cultural apocalypse" a situation where we experience in the most painful way the disintegration of our being-in-the-world and, at the same time, we reconstitute its presence. The empirical manifestations that mark these states of emergency injected in our daily lives are extremely ambivalent: "We need to be careful in noticing that with respect to its "sense" a same behavior can appear to the same individual twice: as the symptom of a crisis and as the sign of a reintegration."[14] The apocalypse stages, in a certain society and in a historically determined culture, the anthropogenetic threshold where we recognize both a "no longer" and a "not yet," an on-going loss and an incipient redemption. It encourages and amplifies the separation between potentiality and actuality, but with the goal of reaffirming their usual connection. When we live through a cultural apocalypse, we experience both a "lack of semanticity" (accompanied by its stereotyped behaviors and signal-like sentences) and a spectacular "excess of semanticity that cannot be expressed by specific meanings" (thus the prevalence of inchoate potentialities). However, both lack and excess are tasked with the restoration of the peculiar conditions of possibility for human discourse.

I will give a simple but fitting example: a grown man, in a moment of despair, talks loudly to himself. This monologue resembles in many important ways the equally extroverted and noisy monologues used by the child to communicate his or her own mastery of the linguistic faculty. The child engaged in "egocentric" litanies and fabulation attains self-consciousness by experiencing him or herself as a source of enunciations (not at all because of what he or she is saying). Similarly, the troubled adult reconstitutes his or her own "synthetic unit of apperception" by staging him or herself as linguistic animal (and not at all by virtue of the occasional semantic contents verbalized in such speech). The external monologue is ambivalent, like every cultural apocalypse: it is a step back in the ontogenetic development, but also its invigorating repetition. Another example falls closer to the phenomena studied by De Martino: the importance attributed to glossolalia by many religious traditions. The compulsive emission of meaningless sentences signals a fissuring of presence. However, isolating the speech act from any communicative intent, the glossolalic speaker goes back to the conditions for any real communication: the ability to produce articulated sounds, the familiarity with the empty phonemes that make meaningful morphemes possible; in short, the pure and simple *potentia loquendi.* With its executions for voice only, the monologist is engaged in a "ritual iteration of the absolute beginning."[15] Even for glossolalia, then, we can embrace De Martino's observation that the same behavior can appear either as the "symptom of a crisis" or as a "symbol of restoration."

The origins coincide with the permanent conditions: this is what founds the constant oscillation between crisis and repetition of anthropogenesis. But this oscillation, besides being infinite, is so frequent and rapid that the two poles are almost indiscernible. Recession and restoration are not only interdependent, but are juxtaposed to the point of seeming co-extensive and concomitant. The crisis is already repetition, and the repetition is not really different from the crisis. Presence is not like a star endowed with autonomous traits, which would temporarily eclipse itself and then reappear: it is entirely dependent on the oscillatory motion between loss and redemption, it rests fully in their indiscernibility. There is no *anthropos* outside the crisis/repetition of anthropogenesis. A cultural apocalypse reveals, or at least vividly recapitulates the biological *semel*-nativity of the human animal. The celebration of this *semel*-nativity was once the prerogative of religious rituals, and now it permeates the entirety of the everyday life in contemporary societies, as we will soon show. We can easily recognize it, like a physiognomic trait. The apocalypse is ubiquitous and explicit. Today, its trumpets are heard in the most common behaviors and enunciations.

Part 2

Toward a Critic of Interiority

> The ultimate goal might very well be for the whole of our internal world to become visible in the external world.
>
> — Friedrich W. J. Schelling

> The gift of language could be seen as proof that man is naturally endowed with a tool capable of transforming the invisible into an appearance.
>
> — Hannah Arendt

> Prior to all the functions aimed at the conservation of the individual and of the species, there is the simple fact of appearing as self-exhibition.
>
> — Adolf Portmann

4

Second-degree Sensualism

A Physiognomic Project[1]

1. Final sensations

Any truly naturalist philosophy is a commentary (and not always unconsciously)[2] of a verse in John's Gospel, "and the Word became flesh." These unprejudiced but sympathetic commentaries can proceed along two lines.

The first one, which I won't pursue in my discussion, consists in emphasizing the physical realities *contributing to* human elocution. Verbal language is possible thanks to a specific bodily configuration: erect station, width of the upper laryngeal tract, fleshy and movable tongue. It is a good thing to celebrate the physiological roots of apophantic speech, recognizing in the voice the transcendental presupposition of all semantic subtlety. Following John, it would be easy to rebut those self-described materialists who oppose the desiring body to a surreptitiously disembodied *logos* that has been made to appear frail and impalpable.

The second direction, which I will take, consists instead in focusing on the physical reality *produced by* human elocution. In this case, the naturalist gloss to the evangelic sentence addresses the corporal effects of the word: they talk about the visual, aural and tactile experience that language makes possible. Sometimes, it isn't only the foundation of our propositions that is physical, but also their results. In many cases the most vivid perceptions are anticipated and prepared by verbal thought: if certain words had not been said we would not have felt them at all. In the following pages I will clarify the status of the sensations constituting the outermost part, or the last section, of a fully deployed linguistic practice. I will call them *final sensations.*

This interpretation of John's verse wants to resolve the impasse crippling philosophical sensualism, which fails when it tries to deduce a verbal concept—such as the concept of negation or of melancholia—from a physical experience. It could, however, score a valuable victory if it focused on analyzing the perceptions *resulting from* verbal concepts; for instance, the physical consequences of words like "no" and "melancholia." Its more ambitious goal is to show that the happy end of a logical inference often is a new direct perception. Sensualism, if we take it seriously, is *everything but* an *incipit* or a quiet foundation. Rather, we need consider it as the crowning point of propositional thought: it is a complex end for quite sophisticated intellectual performances.

We should then investigate the sensible experience that finds in language its *conditions of possibility*. The experience that can be brought about by affirmations, calculations or metaphors; that accompanies and implies the use of words and depends on it. Even if it is the result of logical sequences, such an experience is still immediate. It creates the field of *an aesthetics* that—to say in Kantian jargon—does not found, but is actually posterior to *an analysis*. We could also say that this is a sensualism in the second degree, meaning that perception (tactile, visual and so forth) is completely inconceivable without a previous familiarity with a whole set of verbal concepts. In other words: I call sensations of the first degree a toothache, and of the second degree the sense of an excessive liquidity in the word "flower bed,"[3] or in seeing a sad face in an oval drawing. Second-degree sensualism assumes non-linguistic elements that are, however, radically *post-linguistic*. In this respect, it obeys the Hermetic principle: the lowest is also the highest; the most basic sensual contact is later found as the extreme outcome of logically structured thought.

Only a second-degree sensualism can posit a direct connection between word and sensible world. Only in its sphere enunciations and perceptions cease to belong to parallel series that can only entertain, at best, a complex relation based on translation. In second-degree sensualism it is not the sensible word that evokes the corresponding word, but, on the very contrary, it is the word that institutes its own sensation. It is the adjective "sad" that allows us to recognize immediately a sad expression or to hear in a melody a plaintive and heart-breaking tone.

It seems to me that a sensualism in the second-degree, that is, the elaboration of an *aesthetics* to be placed after an *analytics*, was adequately developed in the second part of the *Philosophical Investigations* (and particularly in chapter XI), where Wittgenstein repeatedly mentions those sensations that could not be felt without the "mastery of a technique." Over two centuries ago, Condillac imagined a statue deprived of any sort of idea and that at first starts to know the world only through the sense of smell, gradually introducing hearing and then all the other senses. Wittgenstein proceeds in the opposite way. Since the human animal is endowed with language, it has from the very beginning all sorts of ideas: what we need to ask is which immediate perceptions are supported and introduced by our semantic competence. We could say that Wittgenstein is concerned with the instances when the sensation of smelling a rose (that was the beginning of Condillac's mental experiment) is not a prelude, but the culmination and the goal of a thought.

In the first part of this chapter I will try to focus on some aspects of the sensations produced by a set of verbal significations. In the second, I will comment on a sentence by Wittgenstein that seems to provide us with a kind of *linguistic physiognomy* whereby "the physiological is the symbol of the logical."

2. Assertion and contact

Wittgenstein anticipates the possibility of a second-degree sensualism when he talks about "a modified concept of sensation":

> We react to the visual impression differently from someone who does not recognize it as timid (in the *full* sense of the word).—But I do not want to say that we feel this reaction in our muscles and joints and that this is the 'sensing.'—No, here we have a modified concept of *sensation.*[4]

How does this change the concept of seeing or hearing? "One cannot mention a sense-organ for this 'sense.'"[5] It does not have a physiological foundation. The eyes of someone who cannot recognize the shyness expressed by a certain face are not defective. Wittgenstein refuses also the thesis (very important in art history) that attributes the recognition of an expression characteristic of someone's physiognomy to empathy, defined as a muscular contraction or some other receptive alteration. What is happening then? When I tie the immediate perception of someone's sadness to a certain sensorial apparatus or even to more than one ("sadness I can hear as much as I can see it"[6]), I am not referring to the information collected by a certain organ, but about the inextricable combination between the latter and verbal thought. When I say "I see your sadness," I denote the part as the whole. This sensation, adds Wittgenstein, "seems half visual experience, half thought."[7] Although as modified concept, it is nonetheless a sensation. A happy face is perceived as an undivided object, not as an oval figure for which the attribution of happiness is true. The impression we have of that face is—in the strong, that is, logical sense—*undeniable*. Perceived happiness, being undeniable, is not to be valued in terms of truth. In this regard, Aristotle's argument in book IX of *Metaphysics* is absolutely appropriate: when talking about simple objects (*ta asuntheta*), he asks "what is being or not being, and truth or falsity." If for composite objects it is clear that a right definition corresponds to the truth and a wrong one to falsehood, for non-composite ones things are different: for them "truth or falsity is as follows:—contact and assertion [*thigein* and *phanai*] are truth (assertion not being the same as affirmation), and ignorance is non-contact."[8] And indeed, a melancholic expression is a "simple thing" (that is, non-composite), whose truth consists in a direct contact and in an enunciation, not in a predicative assertion. When looking at an ambiguous figure (a duck that can also be seen as a rabbit) I suddenly perceive the aspect that previously I had not recognized and I say: "It's a duck." Similarly, when in a puzzle I finally perceive a human profile and I say: "This is what it was!" I don't say anything that's true or false, but I simply engage in *thigein* and *phanai*. "If you search in a figure (1) for a figure (2), and then find it, you see (1) in a new way. Not only can you give a new kind of description of it, but noticing the second figure was a new visual experience."[9]

3. Mastering a technique

Second-degree sensualism (that is, "a modified concept of sensation") is based on the familiarity with a grammar, with a knowledge, with a certain language game. Wittgenstein writes:

> "Now he's seeing it like this," "now like that," would only be said of someone capable of making certain applications of the figure quite freely. The substratum of this experience is the mastery of a technique.
>
> But how queer for this to be the logical condition of having such and such an experience! After all, you don't say that one only 'has a toothache' if one is capable of doing such-and-such.[10]

In the difference between having a toothache and perceiving a triangle now as a hole and now as an arrow,[11] in the hiatus separating these two "lived experiences," we can clearly recognize the difference between first and second-degree sensualism. The variable sensation of the triangle is a second-degree one between which we have the echo of a thought. The lived experience of a toothache is subjective and incommunicable as such, but the lived experience of seeing a triangle drawn in ever-changing ways is based on an objective, public thought. Frege distinguishes between representation (the toothache) and an impersonal thought that would be valid independently from the agreement of specific individuals (the geometrical properties of a triangle). Wittgenstein, however, delineates a third possibility: since the different ways in which we can perceive a triangle (as a hole, an arrow, a painting and so on) would not be possible without the mastery of the concept-triangle, we have to examine the case of a representation that *presupposes* thought, or, in other words, the sensible perception *of* a thought. He writes that "you can think now of *this* now of *this* as you look at it, can regard it now as *this* now as *this*, and then you will see it now *this* way, now *this*."[12]

Another example of the mastery of a technique is the speaker's ability to appreciate separately the vowels, as simple phonological units. This is an important example, because it contains *in nuce* the potentially decisive considerations on the physiognomy, or the "aroma," of words. In Wittgenstein's *Brown Book* we read:

> Consider this case. We have taught someone the use of the words "darker" and "lighter." He could, e.g., carry out such an order as "Paint me a patch of colour darker than the one I am showing you." Suppose now that I said to him: "Listen to the five vowels *a, e, i, o, u* and arrange them in order of their darkness." He may just look puzzled and do nothing, but he may (and some people will) now arrange the vowels in a certain order (mostly *i, e, a, o, u*). [...]
>
> Now, if such a person was asked whether u was '*really*' darker than e, he would almost certainly answer some such thing as "It isn't really darker, but it somehow gives me a darker impression."[13]

With regard to attributing a color to vowels, Wittgenstein says something that is true of all second-degree sensations:

> Here one might speak of a 'primary' and 'secondary' sense of a word. It is only if the word has the primary sense for you that you use it as the secondary one. [...] The secondary sense is not a 'metaphorical' sense. If I say 'For me the vowel e is yellow' I do not mean: 'yellow' in a metaphorical sense,—for I could not

express what I want to say in any other way than by means of the idea 'yellow.'[14]

The same is true for our fondness of qualifying the days of the week as 'fat' or 'lean,' or for using the verbs 'to see' and 'to hear' in sentences like 'see the sadness' and 'hearing the melancholy of a sonata.' A secondary meaning relies on the previous familiarity with a grammar, that is, with certain concepts and techniques, while a primary meaning doesn't. The crucial point is that the secondary meaning is not simply a similitude or a metaphor. If it were so, I could immediately go back to the corresponding literal expression, shifting from poetry to prose. But this is not at all possible: the literal expression does not exist. The yellow of the vowel "e," the skeletal aspect of Tuesdays, the melancholy of a sound: this is the only way of saying what we mean. It is a second-degree meaning referring to a second-degree sensation. It is not a provisional stand-in and can't be changed at will, since it relies on an immediate perception.

It is barely necessary to mention that the distinction between 'primary' and 'secondary' meanings and the fact that the 'secondary' one is not a metaphor are essential to the analysis of ethical propositions made by Wittgenstein in the conference that he gave in Cambridge in 1930 for the circle of the "Heretics." When I say "I wonder at the existence of the world" or "I am safe, nothing can injure me whatever happens,"[15] I am not using words in their ordinary sense. But this does not mean that I am using them as metaphors: what I want to express can only be expressed in those sentences. The same consideration applies to sentences like "having tact" or "this man's life as a value": these are secondary meanings, but they are not metaphors. Ethics, therefore, falls within the realm of second-degree sensualism. The "good life" is a *derived sensation.*

4. Perceiving the properties of a concept

In Part II of the *Philosophical Investigations*, we read at the very beginning of chapter XI:

> Two uses of the word "see." The one: "What do you see there?"—"I see this" (and then a description, a drawing, a copy). The other: "I see a likeness between these two faces"—let the man I tell this to be seeing the faces as clearly as I do myself. The importance of this is the difference of category between the two 'objects' of sight.[16]

An essential reference to understand this "difference of category" (as well as the general concept of "modified sensations") is paragraph 53 of Frege's *Foundations of Arithmetics*. In this text, Frege introduces a distinction between the "characteristics" of a concept (the predicates pertaining to the object relevant to the said concept) and its "properties" (to the predicates pertaining the concept as such):

> By properties which are asserted of a concept I naturally do not mean the characteristics which make up the concept. These latter are properties of the things which fall under the concept, not of the concept. Thus 'rectangular' is not a property of the concept 'rectangular triangle'; but the proposition that there exists no rectangular equilateral rectilinear triangle does state a property of the concept 'rectangular, equilateral, rectilinear triangle'; it assigns to it the number nought. In this respect, existence is analogous to number. Affirmation of existence is in fact nothing but denial of the number nought. Because existence is a property of concepts the ontological argument for the existence of God breaks down. But oneness is not a component characteristic of the concept

> 'God' any more than existence is. Oneness cannot be used in the definition of this concept any more than the solidity of a house, or its commodiousness or desirability, can be used in building it along with the beams, bricks and mortar.[17]

The *component characteristics* of the concept "Paolo's face" are: a nose of a certain dimension, a mouth shaped in such and such a way, two big ears and so on. The *properties* of this concept are its existence, its uniqueness, but also its possible resemblance to someone else's face. The logically decisive difference, according to Frege, between a concept's known characteristics and its properties, is the equivalent of the two uses for the word "seeing" mentioned by Wittgenstein: "I see this thing (and then a description, a drawing, a copy); "I see a resemblance between these two faces." But in Wittgenstein's case this is not a game (as for Frege) nor a subtle philosophical distinction, but a direct perception, a simple visual sensation.

Frege acknowledges that in certain cases it is possible to deduce the properties of a concept (such as number, existence, relation, equivalence) from the perception of its known characteristics, but he underscores the indirect and delayed character of this deduction: "this can never be so direct a matter as it is to assign some component of a concept as a property to an object falling under it."[18] In Wittgenstein's examples, however, there is no diachronic interval between the apprehension of the known characteristics and of the properties of a certain concept. Nor does the intensity vary. With the traits of a face, which are formed in such and such a way, I also perceive with equal immediacy its resemblance with the face of someone else, its uniqueness (if I recognize it as belonging to a person that I used to know and had forgotten), its characteristic ironic reserve. At the moment I see it (and not later, through reflection) I immediately apprehend a predicate of the concept. "What I perceive in the dawning of an aspect is not a property of the object, but an internal relation between it and other objects."[19] This "internal relation," which certainly does not pertain to the object as such but to the way we think about it, "dawns on us" all the same, with irrefutable and immediate evidence. To perceive a house as being cozy, or the uniqueness of Eleonore's face, is "the expression of a new perception and at the same time of the perception's being unchanged."[20] This perception, both new and unchanged, is still a *thigein*, a direct contact, *knowledge by acquaintance*.[21]

Another case when we have the "lived experience" of the properties of a concept, different from those examined by Wittgenstein, is perhaps worth mentioning. I am speaking about caricatures. Let's take, for instance, the famous drawings by Charles Philipon, called *Les Poires* (1834, *The Pears*), which portray the King Louis-Philippe as a pear. The known characteristics of a certain object (Louis Philippe's face) are represented in a way that expresses its equivalence to a fruit epitomizing stupidity. This equivalence is a property of the concept "Louis Philippe," not an attribute of the object. However, in the caricature, the property of "being equal to" is directly manifested: we perceive it vividly and immediately, just as we do a sunset or a pebble.

The caricature is not a casual or arbitrary example of what we mean as second-degree sensualism. We should not overlook the fact that chapter XI of part II of the *Philosophical Investigations* addresses—sometimes in technical detail—several important issues in painting that were often analyzed by art critics and the artists themselves. This chapter, which had started with the theme of the resemblance between two faces, ends with the evocation of the possibility of fixing on a canvas the simulation of a loving glance: “If I were a very talented painter I might conceivably represent the genuine and the simulated glance in pictures.”[22] A necessary counterpoint to the reading of Wittgenstein's observation is Gombrich's essays in his 1959 book *Art and Illusion. A Study in the Psychology of Pictorial Representation.* Let's take, for instance, “Psychology and the Riddle of Style,” where Gombrich discusses the ambivalent figure of the duck-rabbit or “The Experiment of Caricature,” where he examines the perception of the same basic sketches of the human face that appear in Wittgenstein's *Brown Book* and *Philosophical Investigations.* This is not the place to fully account for these intertextual resonances. But we should notice that Gombrich—like Alberti, Vasari, Hogarth and Daumier before him—talks with remarkable philosophical assurance about colored vowels and other forms of synesthesia, the mastery of a technique as necessary condition for the most immediate visual experiences (“the discovery of appearances was due not so much to a careful observation of nature, as to the invention of pictorial effects”[23]), or the “imponderable evidence” guiding an art connoisseur (or, for Wittgenstein, a connoisseur of men). And most of all, Gombrich discusses at length the parallels and the divergences between physiognomic perception and verbal communication.

5. The physiological as symbol of the logical

The essential remark by Wittgenstein on second-degree sensualism is a sentence that we have already quoted as it sums up concisely many other affirmations: “Here the physiological is the symbol of the logical.” The point is that usually we think that verbal language reproduces a previous sensorial schematization of our environmental context, but now we have to consider the opposite situation, that is, the possible sensorial re-elaboration of a previous linguistic schematization.

What follows is a comment in the margins of Wittgenstein's sentence, an attempt to elaborate on its different meanings and implications. First of all, we should talk, however briefly, about Wittgenstein's use of the term *Symbol*, which in the *Tractatus Logicus-Philosophicus* was the equivalent of *Ausdruck*, "expression." The symbol or expression is the sense shared by a class of propositions.[24] A sign can signify different symbols (think about "shift" or "turn"), just as different signs can signify the same symbol ("unmarried man" and "bachelor"). In fact, in language we are always dealing with signs, and not with a symbol itself: "The sign is what is perceivable of the symbol through the senses."[25] In the light of this older definition, how can we read the statement that "the physiological is the symbol of the logical"? Maybe we can say that in certain language games the symbol (as ultimate sense) is apprehended through "physiological" performances that complete and extend verbal communication, such as noticing the resemblance between two faces, identifying a deceiving look, attributing a color to vowels and so on. The same enunciation can correspond to different physiological "symbols": "I see that figure!" (when one recognizes a face where another person can only see a scrawl). Inversely, several enunciations can refer to the same visual or aural "symbol": "this doesn't sound right," or "this sounds like a like to me." Paraphrasing proposition 3.32 of Wittgenstein's *Tractatus*, we could say that in this kind of language games, *the symbol is what is perceivable in the enunciation only through the senses.*

It is not hard to understand how Wittgenstein's statement is a formidable synthesis of the entire physiognomic tradition. The "physiological" is a bodily appearance, an expression, a face; the "logical" stands for what the physiognomists have called character, destiny, or intentionality. The question raised, among other considerations, by Wittgenstein's affirmation would be the following: how can we create a truly philosophical concept of physiognomy that would no longer be dismissed as an eccentric, recreational amusement and would be regarded as a crucial category of thought, comparable to those of "induction," or "a priori"?

It goes without saying that if we want to elaborate a philosophical notion of physiognomy we have to be smart enough to set aside the majority of the existing literature on this topic. We need to find analyses and reflections that, while apparently discussing something else, raise the question of the *face*, or, if we prefer, of the *incarnation* of "logics." Insofar as the pages by Wittgenstein that we have been reading propose a physiological *parousia* of verbal thought, they also point the way to a subtle and innovative notion of physiognomy.

6. Recognizing a face, understanding an enunciation

The pages written by Wittgenstein during the last fifteen years of his life are full of physiognomic themes, terms and most of all examples. Here are some quotations, just to familiarize ourselves with his language:

> I contemplate a face, and then suddenly notice its likeness to another. I see that it has not changed; and yet I see it differently. I call this experience "noticing an aspect."[26]
>
> I meet someone I have not seen in years; I see him clearly, but fail to know him. Suddenly I know him, I see the old face in the altered one. I believe that I should do a different portrait of him now if I could paint.

> Now, when I know my acquaintance in a crowd, perhaps after looking in his direction quite a while,—is this a special sort of seeing? Is it a case of both seeing and thinking? Or an amalgam of the two, as I should almost like to say?[27]
>
> The aspect presents a physiognomy which then passes away. It is almost as if there were a face there which at first I imitate, and then accept without imitating it.[28]

Beyond the countless lexical suggestions, I believe that we can find three major physiognomic themes in Wittgenstein: a) the parallel between the way we recognize a face and how we understand an enunciation; b) the unmistakable physiognomy that a word seems to possess as material signifier, as an acoustic or graphic entity; c)the gestural aspect of language (not to be confused with the language of gestures) that was alluded to by Socrates' sentence: "Speak, so that I can see you."

Let us start with the first issue. Wittgenstein thinks that the physiognomic identification of a known person functions like the understanding of a verbal enunciation. We could say that this identification is the physiological symbol of a logical understanding. This correlation demystifies the erroneous belief that face recognition and verbal comprehension consist of mysterious mental processes that are independent from the traits of the face or, respectively, from the words we hear. The physiognomic approach is therefore adopted in a polemical mode. Let us follow in detail the argument presented in a strategic passage of the *Brown Book*:

> We may shed light on all these considerations if we compare what happens when we remember the face of someone who enters our room, when we recognize him as Mr. So and So,—when we

compare what really happens in such cases with the representation we are sometimes inclined to make of events. For here we are often obsessed by a primitive conception, viz., that we are comparing the man we see with a memory image in our mind and we find the two to agree. I.e., we are representing "recognizing someone" as a process of identification by means of a picture (as a criminal is identified by his photo).[29]

According to Wittgenstein, mnemonic images, whose existence we cannot doubt, present themselves "before our mind immediately *after* having recognized someone."[30] After, not before: first of all I recognize a guy as someone I know, and only later I remember "as he stood when we last saw each other ten years ago."[31] Recognizing a long lost friend is not the consequence of a comparison between what I am looking at now and a previous mental model, since "no such mould or comparison enters into our experience."[32] The only thing that we rely upon is the physiognomy that is standing before us.

Wittgenstein compares the physiognomic reception of a face to the no less physiognomic reception of a musical melody:

> The same strange illusion which we are under when we seem to seek the something which a face expresses whereas, in reality, we are giving ourselves up to the features before us—the same illusion possesses us even more strongly if repeating a tune to ourselves and letting it make its full impression on us, we say "This tune says something," and it is as though I had to find what it says. And yet I know that it doesn't say anything such that I might express in words or pictures what it says. And if, recognizing this, I resign myself to saying "It just expresses a musical thought," this would mean no more than saying "It expresses itself."—"But

> surely when you play it you don't play it anyhow, you play it in this particular way, making a crescendo here, a diminuendo there, a caesura in this place, etc."—Precisely, and that's all I can say about it, or may be all that I can say about it. [...] But in most cases if someone asked me "How do you think this melody should be played?," I will, as an answer, just whistle it in a particular way, and nothing will have been present to my mind but the tune *actually whistled* (not an image of *that*).[33]

Now we come to the decisive passage: the understanding of an enunciation—just like the successful recognition of a human face or the right way of perceiving a musical melody—is not founded on previous (or simultaneous) mental images. It doesn't imply anything more than the enunciation itself. Verbal language possesses a face (that is, an aspect) too, and this is all we can grasp, recognize and *comprehend.*

> What we call "understanding a sentence" has, in many cases, a much greater similarity to understanding a musical theme than we might be inclined to think. But I don't mean that understanding a musical theme is more like the picture which one tends to make of oneself of understanding a sentence; but rather that this picture is wrong, and that understanding a sentence is much more like what really happens when we understand a tune than at first sight appears. For understanding a sentence, we say, points to a reality outside the sentence. Whereas one might say "Understanding a sentence means getting hold of its content; and the content of a sentence is *in* the sentence."[34]

Summing things up: the way we grasp the traits of a face, or of a musical theme, symbolizes the understanding of verbal language.

This relation, however, can also be retraced in the opposite sense, that is: a high level of physiognomic perception—in other words, the perception of shyness or of a subtle deception—is only made possible *by verbal language*, by the ability of understanding an enunciation. There are rather complicated facial expressions that we understand immediately only because we are used to significations, sayings, metaphors and metonymies.

7. The physiognomy of words

The highest level of second-degree sensualism (or, in other words, of a truly philosophical approach to physiognomy) is found when the word itself becomes the object of sensation. It is quite known that in certain pathologies the speaker is obsessed with the material (graphic-acoustic) characteristics of the verbal sign. He can't finish the sentence becomes he or she is hypnotized by the exorbitant number of vowels contained in the name "Paolo," or by the time it takes to pronounce the verb "*arrugginire*."[35] This also happens to the child savoring the meanings of echolalic repetition. The poet's experience is not that different. Wittgenstein describes this phenomenon in a very suggestive way, extending it to all speakers:

> The familiar physiognomy of a word, the feeling that it has taken up its meaning into itself, that it is an actual likeness of its meaning [...] And how are these feelings manifested among us?—By the way we choose and value words.
>
> How do I find the 'right' word? How do I choose among words? Without doubt it is sometimes as if I were comparing them by fine differences of smell: That is too..., that is too...,—this is the right one.—But I do not always have to make

> judgments, give explanations; often I might only say: "It simply isn't right yet." I am dissatisfied, I go on looking. At last a word comes: "That's it!" Sometimes I can say why. This is simply what searching, this is what finding, is like here.[36]

According to Wittgenstein, there are instances when a word shows a familiar aspect and seems the exact portrait of its meaning. We could also say that the word has a face, or even that *it* is a face, when we can no longer separate the signifier from the signified. In the terms used by Franco Lo Piparo in an important essay, this happens when we fully perceive, without any sort of filter, the original *mono-faciality* of the sign. Or, in other words, when its bi-facial appearance (sound and concept, signifier and signified) recedes and vanishes, revealing its true nature as "didactic fiction." Lo Piparo writes that "Signifier and signified … are the dynamic points of a unitary universe that is unitary not because it becomes such, but because it is born that way. As the universe is mono-facial, we cannot distinguish an internal and an external side in it."[37]

When the signifier absorbs its own meaning (in other words, when its mono-faciality is apparent to the naked eye), the word fully exhibits its constitutive corporeal nature. The signifier is the face of language, but we have to add that in this face we can and must find all of its aspects. Meaning should be considered, at best, a particular physiognomic tonality of the word as sensible object. One could object that the material sign still guarantees the visibility of an invisible semantic content, but then we might ask what allows us to believe that this invisible content existed *before* having achieved visibility. At most, we could consider the concept-*signifié* as a trait of the face-*signifiant* that had previously been neglected. This is not different from what happens when we encounter the ambiguous figure studied by Wittgenstein: now you see the duck but not the rabbit, now the rabbit but not the duck; however, there is only one drawing.

8. "Speak, that I may see thee"

This is our last variation on Wittgenstein's theme, "the physiological is the symbol of the logical." We need, however, to make a short digression.

Lichtenberg opposed to Lavater's practice of physiognomy, which was entirely focused on humanity's fixed traits, a detailed analysis of variable traits, such as mimics and gestures, that he called *pathognomy*. I believe that this difference is very important to the understanding of Wittgenstein's reflections on physiognomy, and in fact we know that he deeply appreciated Lichtenberg's work.

In Lavater, physiognomy has a religious grounding: as the invisible God made himself manifest in Christ's human features, so each human being reveals in the structure of his or her face his otherwise hidden interiority. Lichtenberg, instead, pays attention to the most variable and mercurial aspects of human behavior: the physical expression of fleeting emotions, of course, but also recurrent expressions, linguistic tics and mistakes. His attention shifts incessantly between the language of gestures and the gesturality of language. While Lavater collects silhouettes, Lichtenberg looks for word plays, verbal attitudes, proverbs, idiomatic expressions, jokes and rhetorical tropes. He proposes to discover the "physiognomic rules" of language, when he says that by association, it may happen that a word becomes a face and a face a word.

As *physiognomist* of language, Wittgenstein spans the distance between Lavater and Licthenberg: he moves from fixed to variable traits, from the physiognomy of the *Tractatus* to the pathognomy of the *Investigations*, from language as image to language as gesture. Using a distinction introduced by Johann Engel with regard to actors, we can say that at first Wittgenstein considers the proposition as a "pictorial" (that is, reproductive) gesture, and later as an "expressive" (that is, mimic) one. The end of this trajectory can be defined with some accuracy by the sentence that Lichtenberg attributes to Plato: "Speak—said Socrates to Carmides—that I may see thee."

Speak, that I may see thee. Traditional physiognomy opposes this position, since its reason of being resides in denying that the human being finds in linguistic communication a privileged access to truth. However, there is a physiognomy of language that fully appreciates Plato's apocryphal sentence (invented by Lichtenberg himself). Since your speech is already a gesture, a behavior, a mimicry, only when you speak can I grasp your sensible aspect (and even your toothache). If you don't speak, I can't even recognize the true nature of your face. This is not at all a metaphoric recognition (we should remember Wittgenstein's specification: the secondary meaning of a word is not at all metaphorical): when you speak, I see you in the full sense of the word, that is, I perceive you immediately, just like I perceive a green and round apple in a single look.

In Wittgenstein, we find two possible, complementary outcomes for a physiognomy of language. Sometimes, the word—which is often the most expressive of gestures and allows us to literally *see* the speaker—needs extra-linguistic gestures to be fully *seen*, those subtle variations of behavior often invoked by the late Wittgenstein. It is of course true that the experience of the human animal is entirely public, in the inextricable unity of a form of life and a linguistic game. But the relation between these two interdependent sides is not always symmetrical. In many cases, linguistic games give a physiognomy to an otherwise unknown *Lebensform*, revealing its texture and nuances. In other circumstances, however, it is the form of life that appears as the explicatory physiognomy of a previously unintelligible linguistic game:

> We learn this when we come into a strange country with entirely strange traditions; and, what is more, even given a mastery of the country's language. We do not understand the people. (And not because of not knowing what they are saying to themselves.) We cannot find our feet with them.[38]

There are two possibilities, then: either language *is* the face that mimics habits, beliefs and idiosyncrasies, or it is an enigmatic totem that *needs* an extra-linguistic face (the familiarity with subtle nuances in behavior) in order to be resuscitated. In both cases, however, our problems in understanding don't depend at all on the existence of a field of existence separate from the realm of appearances, of an interiority: we may not understand certain people, but "not because of not knowing what they are saying to themselves." The problem resides in the fact that a certain proportion of our external reality (the only one we possess) can remain in the shadows. A truly philosophical practice of physiognomy, such as the one attempted by Wittgenstein, does not aim at grasping interiority with the help of visible clues. This task is left to truffle hounds and ghost chasers (an example of this kind of ghost, or truffle, is "intentionality"). Its job is to elucidate an inexpressive appearance with the help of an expressive one. It does not want to go beyond physiognomy, since it considers that a fully exposed physiognomy is the worthy goal of the "work of the concept."

9. "Imponderable evidences" and the return of physiognomy

A second-degree sensualism is the naturalist paraphrase of John's verse, "and the Word became flesh." "Derived sensations," those that only verbal thought makes possible, are fully physiological experiences, with the caveat that here "the physiological is the symbol of the logical." But let us be careful: for Wittgenstein a symbol is not an optional ornament, but the true sense of a proposition.

Final sensations are "imponderable evidences," defined by Wittgenstein as the perceptive impressions that come at the end of a process, when everything has already been said. They live at the outer limit of verbal discourse. We cannot refute them, and this is why they are "evidences," but neither can we use them as proof or symptom of something else, and this is why they are "imponderable":

> Imponderable evidence includes subtleties of glance, of gesture, of tone. I may recognize a genuine loving look, distinguish it from a pretended one [...] But I may be quite incapable of describing the difference. And this not because the languages I know have no words for it.[39]

Second-degree sensualism, which explores "imponderable evidences" in the light of their linguistic presuppositions, seems to overlap with some aspects of traditional physiognomy. Also for the latter the *logos* has become flesh, appearing in the "subtle nuances in behavior." However, more important than these coincidences, we have to remember some radical differences.

Traditional physiognomy is a parody of Christian Revelation: the spirit comes in the world through wrinkles, hair, protuberances. The face bears witness to an invisible personality. We remember those eyes because, through their brazen or sneaky looks, they announce certain thoughts and passions. But while this position does value sensible appearances, it is only as a means to get to "mental representations" or to some other intangible object. Traditional physiognomy is a pseudo-science also because it does not treat the incarnation of the word seriously enough: it considers the flesh as simple stand-in for an ulterior reality, that is, a sign. Second degree sensualism adopts the opposite stance, as it concerns itself only with the sensations that, being the end point of a vast semiotic process, cannot be considered signs of anything else. As we have said, an "imponderable evidence" is not a keyhole that would let out some interior content, but a self-standing conclusion. It does not refer to something higher, since it is the final outcome of a lived experience.

Second-degree sensualism shares the initial impetus of physiognomy: to give dignity and meaning to bodies, faces, to muscular contractions and distensions. But it shares this impetus only insofar as it rejects the entirety of physiognomic tradition. Rather than considering the perception of a face a sign alluding to something other and hidden, second-degree sensualism sees it as "imponderable evidence," as the final outcome of innumerable linguistic descriptions ("sad," "shy," "dissimulate," and so on). Bodily appearance, such as a smile, does not refer to anything else, it doesn't "stand for," it is *beyond the sign*. Saint Augustine would say that we can *frui*—enjoy—a smile, but not *uti*—use it. It is precisely in this *non-semiotic enjoyment of the sensible* that we can recognize a radically antitheological understanding of the "incarnation of the word."

5

In Praise of Reification

1. Asking for compensation

The most diverse schools of thought have violently denigrated the process of reification. This is the result of a failure of thought. Theoretically unjustified, this fury stems from the stubborn superstition that what really counts in the experience of the human animal is invisible, impalpable, internal. This chapter wants to defend the concept of reification from the prejudice surrounding it, and to dispel some real misunderstandings caused by several well-established but misleading linguistic habits. We simply want to show the crucial role that reification could play in a truly unrepentant materialism. The defense does not appeal to the mercy of the jurors, but demands a full absolution, with the addition of a compensation for the damages incurred by the defendant. The reification of the human faculties is not reprehensible, but inevitable and even desirable.

Reification is a dynamic term: it indicates the passage from a state to another, the progressive transformation from internal to external, from hidden to manifest, from an unreachable *a priori* to empirically observable facts. What is at stake is not something given, but *becoming* what is not—or at least does not seem to be—

a thing. What is reified, therefore, is a prerogative of the mind, a logical presupposition, a way of being, a precondition for experience. What becomes a thing, in other words, is what normally allows and regulates the relation of *Homo sapiens* with the things of the world. In Kantian terms, we would say that in the process of reification we are not dealing with the phenomena represented through transcendental categories, but those corresponding to the very existence of the transcendental categories founding all representation. In Heideggerian terms, we would say, instead, that in the process of reification we don't see a "forgetting of being," but its effective remembering. It is the horizon of sense (that is being as being) against which all objects and events become visible at last—or once more—*as* object and event (that is, on the ontic plane).

The outcome of the reification process is a further *res*, previously inexistent or unrecognized, where an important aspect of human nature can coagulate (biological dispositions, cognitive and ethical attitudes, relation to the peculiar vital context that we call "the world," and so on). A faculty or a way of being, when properly reified, can acquire an undisputable appearance: a *res* is always already a *res publica*. The thing resulting from reification is external to the individual's consciousness: it subsists even when it is neither perceived nor conceived (just as 2+3 remains 5 even if no one believes it). The thing lies outside consciousness but it is strictly related to subjectivity. Or rather: the thing lends an empirical semblance to those aspects of subjectivity that systematically elude consciousness precisely because they constitute its *presuppositions* or its *forms*. Using an approximate metaphor, we could say that reification is the picture of someone's back, which gives full visibility to what is located behind one's consciousness.

2. An antidote to fetishism and alienation

Reification is charged with causing, or exasperating, that impoverishment of the person that in modern culture we call alienation. We say that we are robbed of what is peculiarly ours when this becomes an external object, or, conversely, that it becomes an external object when it is taken away from us. I believe this accusation to be without merit. Far from implying each other, alienation and reification are not only complete opposites, but they interact as poison and antidote. Reification is the only antidote for the dispossession caused by alienation. Conversely, an insufficiently reified existence, thought or way of life is to be considered alienated.

I am neglecting, of course, the most important thing: the social and political context of these notions. I am sticking to their logical statute, hoping that its clarification might have some relevance also for their socio-political context. We can rightly speak of alienation when an aspect of our lives, thoughts and practices becomes foreign and unavailable, while at the same time exerting an inexplicable power over us. Well, there is no need to identify the foreignness and unavailability constituting alienation with the external, public, empirical nature of the *res*. On the contrary: often, the *res* is what is most familiar and accessible. The nexus between an impoverished subjectivity and its possible concretization is unwarranted and misleading. The origins of alienation are to be found in what is presented to the human animal as an unreachable but binding presupposition having no sensible physiognomy, so that it forever eludes the world of appearances. Foreign and unavailable are all the conditions that, while founding all experience, *seem* impossible to experience. I will give one classical example: the thinking I permits the representation of all kinds of phenomena but it is said to never become a phenomenon in itself. What is truly alienating is the infinite regression occurring in a happily non-reified interiority: keeping with our example, all reflection on the nature of the thinking I, since it is based on this same I, seems condemned to move further and further back without ever grasping its own object. The exteriority inherent to reification stops and inhibits this regression, so that the image of an *I preceding the I* is replaced by the much more tangible image of an *I outside the I.* When they become things external to consciousness, several aspects of subjectivity cease to be enigmatic and despotic. We could hypothesize that the human animal is able to grasp its most intimate essence only if the latter acquires (or has always possessed) the autonomy of a *res.* Intimacy and objectuality often help each other,

Just as radical, but subtler and less evident, is the opposition between reification and *fetishism.* The institution of the fetish is a polemical response to the alienation inherent to interiority: the soul is invested in a visible and tangible object. But this response is secondary and misleading: rather than reifying the soul, we simply spiritualize the object. Fetishism is the abject and ridicule caricature of reification. The difference between these two ways to satisfy the same need is radical, as is the contrast between fetishism and reification as alternatives to alienation. If we don't understand this contrast and we assimilate the two terms to the point of treating them as synonyms, we will fatally end up defending from reification the alienated interiority just to keep fetishism at bay. Instead, I believe that a total reification of human nature (or of the transcendental presuppositions of human experience) could stop the infinite proliferation of the fetish.

Fetishism consists in assigning to a meaningless object the qualities that only belong to the mind, while reification underscores the objectual aspect of the mind. Fetishism abstracts, that is, makes ominous and unreachable, a sensible object, while reification shows the spatial-temporal reality inhabited by abstraction itself, that is, it proves the existence of *real abstractions*. Fetishism passes the empirical off as transcendental, while reification results in the empirical revelation of the transcendental. If I attribute to a phenomenon the prerogatives that only belong to the a priori categories of representation, I make it into a fetish. But if I am dealing with phenomena that perfectly mirror the logical structure of those same a priori categories, I am faced with a true reification of representational activities. An example of fetishism is the notion of "simple object" elaborated by Bertrand Russell: a certain object can be made simple, or indescribable, by surreptitiously transferring on it the semantic indetermination of the words used to design it, the deictics "this" and "I."[1] An example of reification is the technical reproducibility of the work of art: its tools have appropriated the basic principles of visual perception, the subjective organization of space and several physical and mental dispositions.

The analysis of reification finds its theological precursor in the patristic disputes about the incarnation of Christ. *Et verbum caro factum est*: what matters is not that the spirit, that is, verbal thought, implies as consequences certain sensible phenomena, but that it takes a specific and contingent body without losing any of its distinctive traits. A Word that would not become flesh would be alienating. If the Word is not incarnated, it remains an inaccessible transcendental presupposition, an unconditioned condition that escapes experience while making it possible. But how does the word become flesh, becoming a fact among facts outside consciousness? The danger of a fetishistic answer is very strong. In *De Carne Christi* (XIII, 1) Tertullian remarks that if the body chosen by the Word to show itself to the world was similar to any other body, it would be unrecognizable as body of the Word. "If the soul is flesh, it is no longer soul but flesh; if the flesh is soul, it is no longer flesh but soul [...] Naming the flesh while thinking about the soul is the most twisted of arguments, as is talking about the soul when thinking about the flesh." This double torsion is the hallmark of fetishism. The crucial point, already present in John's Gospel, is that the flesh of the Word does not come from the muck of the Earth, but from the Word itself. The Word becomes flesh by itself, in itself and for itself. Once again: reification only concerns the objectuality of thought, while fetishism replaces thought with an object.

The contrast between fetishism and reification is apparent in two different fields. Firstly, in our biological relation with the environment and in our social relation with the other members of the species, we can either fetishize or adequately reify what precedes or subsumes the individual and cannot be referred to a single I. Secondly, we can either fetishize or reify the way of life of the individual I, or also the kind of reality alluded to by the fatidic proposition "I think." Whether in the public sphere or in the fundamental structures of consciousness, the alternative between fetishism and reification is rooted in the experience of speech, which is at the same time pre-individual and individuating. In the last instance, the critique of fetishism and the apology of reification result in a careful evaluation of the external, phenomenal, objectual nature of human language.

3. The public nature of the soul

Let us resume briefly the memorable analysis of fetishism given by Marx. In the capitalist mode of production, the activities finalized toward the realization of a specific use value are no longer the main focus or the inspiration for the working process. What is prioritized and valued is the abstract element found in all finalized activities: the psycho-physical energy expended by the worker. The temporal duration of this expenditure defines what really matters, that is, the exchange value of commodities. In logical-linguistic terms, we see an inversion between grammatical subject (concrete work, use value) and predicate (work in general, exchange value). The attribute replaces the substance; the consequence becomes the starting point. The most outrageous pretense of idealism finds a practical realization: the genus exists independently from the species; "horsiness" prevails over the single horse. The different kinds of work become the contingent, inessential and therefore degraded manifestations of a work without any qualities. The relations among producers are absorbed by the exchange values of commodities. The commodity can be sociable, enterprising, mocking or reticent with respect to other commodities, and typically human vices and virtues seem to inhere to a yard of fabric or a pound of tobacco. According to Marx, the attribution of human relations to the world of things is fully fetishistic:

> A commodity is therefore a mysterious thing, simply because in it the social character of men's labor appears to them as an objective character stamped upon the product of that labor; because the relation of the producers to the sum total of their own labor is presented to them as a social relation, existing not between themselves, but between the products of their labor. This is the reason why the products of labor become commodities, social things whose qualities are at the same time perceptible and imperceptible by the senses. [...] it is a definite social relation between men

> that assumes, in their eyes, the fantastic form of a relation between things. In order, therefore, to find an analogy, we must have recourse to the mist-enveloped regions of the religious world. In that world the productions of the human brain appear as independent beings endowed with life, and entering into relation both with one another and the human race. So it is in the world of commodities with the products of men's hands. This I call the Fetishism which attaches itself to the products of labor, so soon as they are produced as commodities, and which is therefore inseparable from the production of commodities.[2]

The fetish is both "perceptible and imperceptible by the senses." We will return to this undoubtedly suggestive expression, since it can also be applied to the processes of reification that, far from coinciding with fetishism, are the only effective response to it. And in fact, it is quite intuitive that this expression can be understood in two different and even antithetical ways: it can refer to a sensible being usurping the prerogative of an invisible concept or, inversely, to a metaphysical object finally revealing its sensible reality. Let us consider the fetish par excellence, money. Money is the tangible representative of the labor contained in the commodities, the measure of the different exchange values. But this supremely social function is attributed to the natural materials of which it is made. Marx wonders: "Whence arose the illusions of the monetary system? To it, gold and silver, when serving as money, did not represent a social relation between producers, but were natural objects with strange social properties."[3] The physical-chemical properties of a certain object are transfigured into spiritual qualities, logical attitudes, juridical requisites. This is how an object becomes both "perceptible and imperceptible" to the senses.

Transforming a relation among men into a relation among things: this is one of the main distinctive characters of fetishism. We are left to wonder, however, whether a relation between men, admitting it escapes this dangerous metamorphosis, becomes an intangible mental state or whether it creates its own, non-fetishistic but still external and visible *res*. We can oppose the fetishism of the commodity with an effective reification of social relations, not with the invisible introspection of thoughts and relations. The relation among men, when it remains within the individual conscience, fatally becomes a direct personal dependency: we know this, historically, from the example of pre-capitalist, organic and communitarian societies, where human relations, unmediated by objects, are nonetheless strictly regulated by institutional, corporative and religious institutions. The de-reified internalization of public life is always accompanied by the most violent subjection and the most rigorous "alienation," if we still want to use this term. But if the alternative to fetishism is to be found in reification, and not in the vain murmur of our inner life, we need to carefully specify what constitutes the non-fetishistic objectuality of the social bond.

Reification does not concern the men entering in a relation, but the relation itself. This is what is manifested as *res*, as an array of objects and sensible phenomena. The relation among men, which can never be reduced to a mental representation, is incarnated in the *objects of the relation*. This is very different from its fetishistic transformation in *a relation among objects*. Reification operates on the relation, fetishism on the participants. Therefore there exists, among the two, a logical separation. This is perfectly understandable when we think that fetishism trans-values and spiritualizes a given object, while reification makes extrinsic and objectual an abstract concept (such as class or social relation). In other words: reification acts on the preposition "among," normally overlooked when we talk about human relation. The "among" does not define a single individual, but precisely what, in each human animal, goes beyond the individual, pertains to the species and is shared by all before the emergence of the single "I." The "among" preceding individual consciousness appears as sensible *res*, and insofar as it becomes an external object, what precedes the "I" ceases to dominate it as transcendental presupposition (but also as political and religious hierarchy). Reification de-centers the objects involved in the "among," and poses the "among" as an object.

The reification of relation has been explored with the most depth by a child psychoanalyst, Donald Winnicott, and a philosopher interested both in technology and in the principle of individuation, Gilbert Simondon. Obviously, the theoretical contexts of these two authors are very different, sometimes even impossible to compare. But this is exactly what makes the incontrovertible convergences between them all the more significant.

Both Winnicott and Simondon think that our relation with the world and with other human beings is not rooted in the internal, already individuated "I," but rather in a no-man's land where "I" and "non-I" are still indistinguishable. Winnicott calls it a "potential space" between subject and environment, while Simondon talks about a "preindividual nature" non reducible to self-consciousness. In addition, they both consider that the no-man's land of the "among" (where, according to Winnicott, we spend most of our life) manifests itself in objects and events. These tangible and visible things are neither "mine" nor "yours," as they pertain to what is not, and cannot be, individualized in the subject. These are *res publicae* in the strictest sense of the term, if we call "public" the original state preceding the separation between psychic and social existence. The "among" of the relation, according to Winnicott, shows itself in transitional objects (pillars of culture and play). In Simondon, the same "among" is reified in trans-individual objects (and more particularly in technical objects). Only transitional and trans-individual reifications can escape the fetishism of the commodity.

Winnicott thinks that the first transitional object coincides with the mother's breast. For the newborn, the breast is an intermediate *res* between his own body and the body of someone else, an undifferentiated threshold between a still un-limited self and an environment that has not yet been rejected as non-I. The intermediate res doesn't connect two pre-constituted entities, quite the opposite: it makes possible their subsequent constitution as separate polarities. The relation pre-dates the related terms: at the beginning there is the "among," which is always reified. Transitional objects, the things belonging to the relation, are not the exclusive prerogative of infancy. They remain important throughout our existence: they are not a chronological episode, but a lasting modality of experience for the human animal. For Winnicott, the objects of play are typically transitional. Be it the teddy bear that the child refuses to give up or the cards of the poker player, the masks used in a game of charades or a complicated crossword puzzle, the objects of play make visible the "potential space" between mind and world: this is a subjective but external space, public but not yet social insofar as we call "social" the interactions among people possessing a strongly defined identity.

Transitional objects risk remaining unseen simply because they penetrate into every corner of adult life. They are omnipresent in culture, art, and religion.[4] Creativity and invention set up camp in the border zone between I and non-I that we can call *the public mind* or, in other words, a fully external subjectivity. Cultural products, just like the teddy bear (or in another field the baptism ritual or the Eucharist in the Christian doctrine), lend a body to the pre-personal environment of the "among." They are both perceptible and imperceptible, as transitional objects reifying the original relation among the human animal, its fellow humans and their environment. These objects are both perceptible and imperceptible, but they are not fetishes, since they embody the preconditions of the human relation (the "among" itself) rather than reducing it to the "spectral objectuality" of commodity exchange. In fact, the most reliable accomplices of fetishism are those who anxiously try to purge culture from any objectual residue, failing to recognize the fundamentally public nature of the mind.

Let us consider for a moment Simondon's philosophy of technology. The process of individuation that makes of every human being a unique, discrete entity is always limited and partial; in fact, Simondon considers it infinite by definition. The "subject" transgresses the limits of the "individual" because it contains a non-eliminable component, that is, a certain measure of undetermined pre-individual reality, unstable and yet full of potential. This pre-individual reality coexists with the singular I but is never fully assimilated by it and retains its own autonomous forms of expression. The pre-individual is what founds collective experience, which for Simondon does not consist in the convergence between individuated individuals, but in the various manifestations of what, in a given mind, cannot be individualized. Simondon calls transindividual all that escapes the singular self-consciousness precisely because it constitutes its heterogeneous presupposition, which is pre-individual. The technical object is transindividual to a supreme degree:

> Through the technical object we create an inter-human relation that is the model of transindividuality, defined as a relation that does not connect individuals through individualities previously constituted by separation, nor through what is the same in every human subject, like, for instance, the *a priori* form of sensibility. Rather, transindividuality works through the measure of preindividual reality and natural energy that is preserved in the individual being and is full of potential and virtualities. The object created by technical invention bears the traces of the being that produced it and expresses what in this being is less dependent from a *hic and nunc*. We could say that in the technical object there is something belonging to human nature. The word "nature," here, could be used to describe what is original, even older than a humanity constituted in human beings. Man invents through the utilization of its natural support, of the *apeiron* that still survives in each individual being. No anthropology taking man as individual as point of departure can explain the transindividual technical relation [...]. The inventor is not the individual, but a broader and richer subject who contains, besides the individuality of the individual being, a certain natural charge belonging to the non-individuated being.[5]

The machine gives a spatio-temporal dimension to the collective, species-specific aspects of human thought. The preindividual reality present in the human subject, unable to find an adequate expression in the representations of the individual consciousness, is projected in the external world into systems of universally receivable signs, intelligent machines, logical schemes made *res*. We find again a crucial philosophical issue: thanks to technology, we can see what precedes the individual in the external world. The inaccessible presupposition becomes a post-separation object that can be touched and seen. The machine can also be considered an object that is both perceptible and imperceptible. But differently from the money-fetish, which is both perceptible and imperceptible because important social virtues are attributed to its natural body (be it gold or copper), the machine results from an opposite process, that attributes to a mental structure the autonomous relevance characteristic of sensible objects. Obviously, the trans-individual sphere of experience symbolized and sustained by technology cannot be confused with the psychological realm, but neither can it be identified with the social system. Technical objects, just as the transitional objects studied by Winnicott, define an intermediate region: "Technical activity is neither fully social nor psychological. It is the model of collective relations."[6] In addition, according to Simondon it would be a grave error to consider technology a simple complement of labor processes. Actually, the two terms are symmetrical and heterogeneous: technology is *trans*individual while labor is *inter*individual; the first reifies the "among," while the second is always in danger of becoming fetishistic. "We need a conversion that would allow the human side of the technical object to appear directly, without passing through labor relations. It is labor that needs to be considered but a phase of technology, not the opposite."[7] The latent contrast between labor and technology had been discussed by Marx himself: it is sufficient to think about the famous pages where he attributes to the *general intellect*, that is, to thought as public (or rather, transindividual) resource, the merit of reducing unqualified wage labor to a superfluous remainder.[8]

4. Transindividual words

The transitional and transindividual objects theorized by Winnicott and Simondon reify the "among" that founds all human relations. But we need to take another step and ask ourselves the following question: which *res* incarnates the "potential space" between mind and world earlier and more radically than play and technology, giving an external and sensible aspect to the "preindividual reality" of the human animal? The answer is intuitive: verbal language is the supreme transitional and transindividual object. The reification of the "among," of the relation as such, is always effectuated in our tired, ready-made words. These words, which predate the individuation process of the single person, institute the no-man's (and everyman's) land between the I and the non-I. Historical-natural languages are an external realm that is subjective but does not coincide with the operations of consciousness, public but not equivalent to social roles. In language, the transcendental categories grounding the possibility of experience finally (or more credibly, from the beginning) appear as experiential objects. Reified in a lexicon and a syntax, the collective *a priori* is transformed in an aggregate of empirical facts. It is first and foremost thanks to language that the transindividual presuppositions of the self-conscious I are manifested externally, adapting to the perfectly honorable *status* of phenomena.

Language is by definition "perceptible and imperceptible" at the same time. The conceptual content of the word is inseparable from its acoustic and graphic characterization. In his great essay on the "monofaciality of the sign," Franco Lo Piparo has shown how the distinction between the two planes leads to an impasse all those who conceive the incarnation of the Word in a bi-facial manner: "Only the most tortuous reasoning names the flesh [the audible *signifiant*] when thinking of the body [the incorporeal *signifié*], or designates the soul when talking about the flesh."[9] The monofaciality of the sign, that is, the full coincidence between expression and content indicates very clearly what we mean as "the flesh of words" in a naturalistic context. Verbal thought does not look for any kind of body (this or that articulated sound) trying to become a phenomenon and a *res*, but is already corporeal, phenomenal, objectual. It is one with the work of our lungs and epiglottis which produces sounds.

Our psychological resistance to considering language a sensible, audible and visible *res* corresponds to the fetishistic inclination to attribute to the most disparate objects the prerogatives that are unique to language. Let's remember, for instance, Kafka's Odradek, the unnamed, small moving object that haunts an apartment building creating many problems for the father. This is not different from Russell's "simple object," which has made so much trouble for analytic philosophy. But philosophical Odradeks are famous and innumerable. They owe their existence as fetishes to two related assumptions: first we affirm the autonomy of thought-*signifié* with respect to the body-*signifiant*, and then, on the strength of the presumed bi-faciality of the sign, we transfer certain traits of disincarnated thought-*signifié* to the object that we are talking about (instead of attributing them, as we should, to our words as simple audible *res*).

Another good example is negation. When we unduly detach its conceptual meaning from the word "not," that is, from the body of the signifier, we inevitably end up postulating the existence of beings and facts that would be negative in themselves, and therefore able to negate the existence of other beings and facts. These enigmatic "negative objects" are nothing more than an animistic projection: they are Odradeks to the nth power. If we don't recognize the nature of language as inseparably perceptible and imperceptible, that is, the reification of the mind that language implies, ends up justifying fetishism by attributing a certain kind of conceptual attitude to a non-conceptual object.

Language is the objectual background of thought. Every word is closely related to the notion of *Urphänomen* elaborated by Goethe's: each word is the "original phenomenon" showing in a contingent and empirical manner an idea wrongly considered invisible. Reification, therefore, consists in bringing thought back to the transitional and transindividual objects that constitute language. It resembles an *anamnesis*, a clarifying memory: we remember things that are perceptible and imperceptible at the same time, that is, the audible signifiers that embody the transcendental categories from the very beginning. The essay by Emile Benveniste entitled "Categories of Thought and Language" is a true exercise in reifying anamnesis, where all ten Aristotelian categories are seen in the light of their rigorously linguistic, and sometimes even idiomatic, origin:

> [Aristotle] thought he was defining the attributes of objects but he was really setting up linguistic entities [...] The language did not, of course, give direction to the metaphysical definition of "being"—each Greek thinker has his own—but it made it possible to set up "being" as an objectifiable notion which philosophical thought could handle, analyze and define just as any other concept.[10]

To say that we express our thoughts through words is a familiar but misleading formulation. When we hear it, we might assume that words come last, with the secondary task of manifesting or actualizing pre-existing thoughts. This is not the case. Quite the opposite: be it calculations or metaphysical meditations, *cogitationes* actualize language. A much more meaningful, although apparently paradoxical, statement would be that *we translate our words into thoughts*. Reflection's task is to realize the different opportunities represented by the perceptibly imperceptible, that is, monofacial, signs that dwell in the world of audible and visible appearances.

5. The vicissitudes of the "I think"

At this point, we need to ask ourselves how the individual consciousness experiences the alternative between fetishism and reification. This time, what is at stake is no longer the relation between human beings (and its potential reversal into a relation between things) but what insures the unity of a particular biography in the life of the mind. We are not talking about the intermediate region between I and non-I, but the constitution of the singular I itself. Which fetishistic misunderstandings threaten the subject of self-reflection, that is, the subject who knows, who thinks, who says "I" to designate him or herself? And conversely: what would be an adequate reification for the subject, that is, his or her objectual, phenomenal, empirical correlative? The contrast between fetishism and reification, in this case, concerns the "I think" or, in Kantian jargon, the synthetic unity of apperception. In order to illustrate concisely this contrast, I will use a seminal text of modern philosophy that has influenced a large part of German idealism and later, by adhesion, more than a proposition of Wittgenstein's *Tractatus*. I am referring, of course, to the *Critique of Pure Reason*, where Kant discusses the vicious circles (the technical term is "paralogisms") in which metaphysical psychology gets lost when considering the existence of the self-conscious subject.

The mistake of metaphysical psychologists—but also, let's add just for pleasure of controversy, of many ultra-materialist psychologists who are now filling the ranks of today's philosophy of the mind—consists in wanting to apply to the nature of the self-conscious I notions (such as substance, simplicity, indivisibility and so on) that would not even be conceivable without presupposing … a self-conscious I! The "I think" is the unity without content preceding and allowing the unification of empirical multiplicity through its categories. Kant remarks that it is a fallacy (that is, a "paralogism") to try and grasp conceptually the very foundation of conceptual thinking: "we revolve around it in perpetual circles, since before we can form any judgment about it we must already use its representation."[11] The way of being designated as "I think" is unattainable for the thinking I. The latter can talk easily about his or her empirical person, and of the cognitions and passions that characterize its existence, but in this way it will only be an *object* of representation like any other. The thinking I can say nothing as subject of representation, and this is the issue. "But the identity of the subject of which, in all its representations, I can become conscious, does not concern the intuition of the subject by which it is given as object."[12]

Metaphysical psychology indulges in the most luminous example of fetishism. The condition of possibility for self-consciousness is mistaken for an attribute of the thing perceived. Let us consider more closely how this fetishistic metamorphosis incurred by the self-conscious I (that is no longer the "among" of the subject's preindividual reality) is articulated. The "I think" is a text, a linguistic production: the "only text" (*das einige Text*, says Kant) at our disposal to understand subjectivity. Said text exhibits (or, in other words, continuously reiterates) the formal unity of consciousness on which all representations converge, but it tells us nothing about the conscious being who is the author of such representations. The pretense of deriving from the logical-linguistic characteristics of the proposition "I think" any information on the nature of the I is purely fetishistic. This pretense can be explained thus: since the word "I" is a term that always figures as a grammatical subject, the I is considered an immaterial substance. From the indivisible unity of a representation that directs the verb to only one person we further deduce that the Subject is simple (incorruptible). The fact that "I" recurs in the use that all speakers make of it to designate themselves in the most disparate circumstances is enough to affirm the identity (personality) of the soul. Infra-textual connections and values thus become the qualities of an autonomous entity that can be called "person," "subject" or "the mind."

Let us stick with the most flagrant misunderstanding that anticipates or complements the others: we consider self-consciousness as a *substance*. The I-substance, obtained by mistaking the unity in the synthesis of thought for a unity perceived in the subject of this thought, or, in Kant's words, that "I am for myself a self-subsistent being or substance."[13] This is a fictitious substitute for the "I"-word, which is the only real player *in the proposition* "I-think." The I-substance, this objectual Frankenstein created on the model of self-consciousness, gives a perverse answer to the irrepressible need to determine the mode of being of subjectivity. By itself, this need is far from reprehensible, as it tries to experience the conditions of possibility for experience. The answer, however, is perverse and, more importantly, improbable. The fetishized double of the "I think" is still subjected to it: therefore, it confirms the presupposition that it wanted to transform in something already there. Like all fetishes, the I-substance is disquieting. It shares many prerogatives of the *doppelganger*, that Freud considered one of the figures displaying the uttermost superposition of touching familiarity and frightening uncanniness.

The double, just like the hypostasized subject of Kant's paralogism, can lead to "doubling, dividing and interchanging the self."[14]

The Kantian critique of the "inevitable appearances" ensnaring pure reason when approaching the soul is, in its main aspects, a stringent critique of fetishism. On the other hand, what happens to the I once it emerges from the paralogistic fogs? If we follow Kant, it would seem that the thinking I, which always presupposes its own existence, is presented with a rather melancholic choice when thinking about its own nature: infinite regression or complete ineffability. The pure I can only gesture toward the limit separating it from the non-I, without ever defining what is truly its own domain. We should notice that are attributed to the non-I (according to the extreme but not arbitrary interpretation given by Fichte to Kant's chapter on paralogisms) also the occasional feelings and contingent experiences typical of any individual life. Before talking about some very different conclusions that we could reach on the basis of the confutation of the paralogisms, we should pause for a moment to discuss the ethical vicissitudes of a subject that, in order to avoid fetishism, breaks with the phenomenal field and retreats in an ineffable interiority.

Such vicissitudes are narrated quite vividly by Hegel in his *Introductory Lectures on Esthetics* when he dismantles the theories of the Romantic thinkers Schlegel and Solger, who thought that the pure I (after having rejected Kant's paralogism) has to assume an ironic attitude, that would recognize its own incommensurability with the objects and events of the empirical world. Irony dwells in a self-consciousness deprived of exteriority and marks a Word reluctant to become flesh. The undetermined I, "utterly abstract and formal," considers true only its own productions, but "what is by my favor, I am in turn able to annihilate."[15] The focus of romantic—but also postmodern—irony is the compulsive negation of all that could give an objective image of the I. In order to escape objectification, the subject undoes what it has just done, takes its leave having just been introduced, and mocks what he just said in all seriousness. The infinite regression inevitably awaiting the self-searching subject finds its ethical consequence in the interminable ironic corrosion of every definite experience. The romantic individual (but also the "flexible" man extolled by postmodern thought) shows an ironic jadedness while hoping to find a stable support in a non-reified interiority. According to Hegel, nothing is more improbable: "If the I remains at this point of view, all appears to it as nothing worth and as futile, excepting its own subjectivity, which thereby becomes hollow and empty."[16] The poverty and alienation of a subject determined to avoid fetishism through introspection are extreme and can't be tolerated for a long time: this is why Hegel says it is the ironic I who, most of all, starts to "feel a craving for the solid and the substantial."[17] In other words: the extreme retreat into the self makes the subject vulnerable to the same paralogism (thinking that consciousness is a substance) that he believed to have avoided once for all. The mirage of inner autonomy and the fetishism of the substance feed on each other, determining a perpetual oscillation that some mistake for an irreconcilable contradiction.

The I-substance is not rejected, but rather is justified, by the ineffable, elusive, ironic I. Even with regard to self-consciousness, as it was already the case in human relations, the opposition to fetishism does not consist in the false movements of our inner lives (the I preceding the I) but in its opposite, that is, in a truly perspicuous reification of human nature (the I outside the I). It is true that we cannot apply to the self-reflective subject the categories that it founds, but nothing prevents us from thinking that, if properly understood as the foundation of the categories, this subject has an extroverted and perceptible nature. The "I think" is indeed precategorical, but it is not disembodied, that is, deprived of an objectual aspect. The separation between the paralogistic *quid pro quo* and its confutation is subtle, but decisive, just as the difference between a poison and its antidote. The inclination to treat the transcendental foundation of all representations as any other represented object is in fact fetishistic, but the attempt to analyze the empirical phenomena that make that foundation visible is reifying. The deduction of a I-substance from an I-word is fetishistic, while emphasizing the sensible, evental and in any case extrinsic reality of the I-word is reifying. Against paralogisms, we need to explain in detail the different ways in which the synthetic unit of apperceptions becomes incarnate in a variety of visible and audible *res*. Obviously we are not talking about the things known *by* self-consciousness, but those (in the larger definition of the Latin term, such as objects, facts, and circumstances) who are the support *of* self-consciousness. Finally, what is the *Urphänomen* of the I, that is, the spatiotemporal event that manifests transcendental subjectivity? What is perceptible and imperceptible at the same time, and exhibits the presuppositions for thought?

6. Self-consciousness as performative linguistic act

Kant insists repeatedly, mostly in the first edition of his *Critique*, on the fact that the "I think" is only a preposition, a text, a verbal construct. We should recognize right away that this is the narrow pass that the reification of consciousness needs to cross in order to chase away the fetishistic paralogisms without falling in the infinite regression where irony dwells. To verify this assertion and sharpen our focus, let us look at some quotes (chosen rather arbitrarily among an overabundant catalogue) emphasizing the role of language in transcendental apperception:

> The formal proposition of apperception, I think, remains the sole ground on which rational psychology ventures upon the extension of its knowledge. This proposition, however, is not an experience, but only the form of apperception that adheres and is antecedent to every experience.[18]
>
> I am simple means no more than that this representation, I, does not contain the smallest manifoldness [...] the famous psychological proof is founded merely on the indivisible unity of a representation, which governs only the verb with respect to a person.[19]
>
> The simplicity of the representation of a subject, however, is not therefore a knowledge of the simplicity of the subject itself, because we abstract altogether from its properties when we designate it solely by the entirely empty expression I (which we can apply to every thinking subject).[20]
>
> The identity of the consciousness of myself at different times is therefore only a formal condition of my thoughts [...], and proves in no way the numerical identity of my subject [...], though we may still attribute to it the same name of I.[21]

The propositional nature of the "I think" is more than sufficient to discredit the current legend about Kant's silence with respect to language. The great absent intervenes at the most delicate juncture, when we need to establish the foundation of the whole transcendental system: the unity of consciousness. From this unity depends the very possibility of experience, and it is simply a text, that is, the basic syntactic juncture between a personal pronoun and a verb. However, the prominence attributed to language in the chapter devoted to the paralogisms raises a thorny issue: the text supposed to guarantee the unity of consciousness will still be able to perform its task if it fails to mention explicitly its linguistic nature? Isn't it true that, if this was the case, consciousness would refer to itself only in a partial and imperfect manner? This is the decisive point. If the "I-word" is the true transcendental subject, then we can easily see that there is a blind spot in Kant's understanding of self-reflection, that is, of the initial relation between the I and itself. When we say "I think" concerning ourselves, we use language in order to abstract the precondition of all determined representations, but we don't account for our act of saying: we do not perceive ourselves as speakers. The proposition "I think" doesn't refer at all to its being no more than a proposition. Thus we neglect the final and most decisive presupposition of the I: the loquacity of the human animal, the textual form of its thought. This is why the proposition "I think" cannot be considered the foundation of self-consciousness. When, like Kant, we recognize its linguistic nature, we also come to terms—however paradoxical it might seem—with its loss of authority. The text that institutes and continuously renews the self-referentiality of the subject and its immediate self-awareness has to be different, and much more radical. The synthetic unit of apperception coincides, therefore, with the proposition attributing to the I the linguistic faculty, that is, with the proposition that founds all others ("I think" included). This truly self-reflexive proposition is: "*I speak.*"

When we really want to challenge a text we need to try its status in a concrete discursive situation. What happens when we really enunciate the sentence "I speak"? Articulating these sounds, we don't describe the act of speaking: we execute it. We don't simply account for a state of affairs, but we create it anew just by mentioning it. "I speak" is a *performative enunciation.* It realizes an action. "I speak" resembles fragments of praxis such as "I baptize this child Luca," "The session is open," or "I forgive you": when they speak, the priest, the speaker of the House or the betrayed lover don't talk about what they are doing, but they do something as they speak. There is, however, a clear difference between "I speak" and the usual performatives. The actions of baptizing and of opening a session, while they are realized by a speech act, have a defined content that is not reducible to speech. In the case of "I speak," instead, the action realized with these words is limited to ... speech! We are not dealing with an event realized through language (a baptism, a pardon, a command, a sermon, a wedding and so forth) but the event *of* language, or, if we prefer, language *as* event.

The transcendental apperception coincides with an action during which—to quote the almost proverbial title of John Austin's 1962 book, we do *things with words*. The thing realized when we say "I speak" is the self-attribution of the generic *potentia loquendi*, the indeterminate linguistic faculty. Taking charge of the ability to talk by talking is the foundation of self-consciousness. Self-consciousness, therefore, is something that is realized with words. Rather than opening a session (a determined thing), we inaugurate or reactivate the unity of the subject (the transcendental *thing*). Instead of assigning the name "Luca" to a newborn, we baptize "I" the single living body that is producing a signifying voice. Self-consciousness possesses the form and the prerogatives of a performative enunciation. The pure I, subject to the *a priori* categories organizing thought, most certainly is not a substance, neither is it an ineffable presupposition: it consists in a linguistic act. And a linguistic act can't but be extrinsic, phenomenal, perceptible. If it remained a silent mental representation, the performative enunciation: "I bet a million dollars that the Steelers will win"[22] would be meaningless. The same is true for "I speak": its vocalization is an integral part of its meaning. The laryngeal motion that allows us to perform the locutory action we claim to be realizing is the sensible interface of the synthetic unit of apperception. The voice, which in the speech act "I speak" acquires the status of an indispensable logical requisite, reifies the transcendental subject each and every time. It is the *res*, now harmonious, now strident, of the talking I. Self-consciousness coagulates in articulated sounds, situated in time and space. It has the consistency of an empirical fact, solidly anchored to the world of appearances. The foundation of categorical thought is not a thought, but an action. An audible action.

Since "I speak" is a performative enunciation, that is, an event dependent on the effective use of the phonic apparatus, we need to specify the occasions for its actual appearance. The transcendental role of this proposition is inseparable from its empirical use. The linguistic act "I speak" (differently from the evanescent "I speak") guarantees the synthetic unit of apperception only if it is actually performed. It has to appear under the guise of a familiar, humble statement without any particular distinction. But when does this happen? "I speak" is to be understood as the adequate paraphrase, or the explicit version, of all enunciations whose communicative content has no importance or is absent, while their most remarkable aspect is the one that usually remains unnoticed: the fact of speech and of breaking the silence, the action of talking in itself, the insertion of speech in the world. I have already analyzed in detail the language games where what we say is a simple pretext to signal the fact that we are speaking and the enunciation only communicates that we are indeed producing a sentence. I will only give some explanatory reminders. In the monologues of the small child, the semantic content expressed is not what counts, but rather it is the noisy verification of his or her own linguistic faculty. It is not the text of the enunciations, but the fact of producing them. Freed from its communicative and denotative tasks, the vocalized soliloquy allows the young human being to experiment with its role as originator of statements. The same happens to adults when we engage in those unstructured conversations that we call, with unjustified severity, small talk: when we do so, we simply show that we are taking part in the conversation. The banal or empty nature of the opinions expressed allows us to focus our attention on the speech as such, that is, on the event *of* language. Furthermore, the eclipse of what we say and the concomitant prominence of the fact of speaking characterize religious rituals: we only need to think about the use of dead or foreign languages, or to the value that has often been attributed to glossolalia. In all of these cases, we are actually saying "I speak." That is when we introduce ourselves as linguistic animals, to ourselves and to others at the same time: self-consciousness, far from being a secretive and private occurrence, is inseparable from an extreme self-exposure to the gaze of our fellow human beings. The ways in which we actually prove our ability to speak are indeed common and familiar, and they transform in an empirical experience the transcendental presupposition of every specific representation.

"I think" is a *descriptive* enunciation, since it simply remarks on an indisputable psychic reality. "I speak," instead, is a *performative* enunciation, which, leaving the psychic realm, shares the external nature and the tangible nature of praxis. Both statements are self-reflexive, although to a different extent. "I think," precisely because it is a linguistic text, is not the highest point of self-reflection, but is dependent on the far more radical "I speak." The latter refers to the ability of producing linguistic texts that in the former remains either an implicit premise or a blind spot. The difference between "I think" and "I speak" is not reducible to a difference in degree. It is more than that. The self-referentiality intrinsic to a performative speech act is logically different from the self-referentiality that can occur in a descriptive assertion.

If I say "The session is now open," this statement refers to itself as an action: my words describe the state of affairs that they are creating in the world. We have a virtuous circle between saying and doing, language and praxis. The bi-faced character of the performative enunciation (which is meaning and action at the same time) causes a self-reference that I will call *heterogeneous*. We can think, for instance, of the ambiguous figures studied by the psychology of perception, like, for instance, the drawing that we can perceive either as a duck or as a rabbit. In the performative kind of self-reference, the duck-meaning brings us back to the rabbit-action, and vice versa. And now let's take a classical case of descriptive self-reference: "This statement is false." The enunciation talks about itself, but only *as enunciation*. It asserts something about its own semantic requisites. Now the drawing is divided between the figures of two indistinguishable ducks, with each being called to account for the other. We are dealing with a homogeneous self-reference. And a homogeneous self-reference is never conclusive: on the contrary, it is destined to infinite regression. The enunciation that describes it, since it is identical to the enunciation it describes, will also need to be described. But the complete homogeneity between *designans* and *designatum* causes the new description to require another one, and so on, without end. The self-reference caused by a proposition describing itself as such is analogous to the interminable regression of metalanguages, which, as it is well known, degenerate very quickly in a language-object.

The reflexivity of "I think" is analogous to the one of "This enunciation is false"; the reflexivity of "I speak" brings to its apex the virtuous circle demonstrated by "The session is now open." When correctly understood, the Cartesian cogito means: *cogito me cogitare*, I think about myself thinking. The descriptive enunciation "I think," as soon as we analyze it with some rigor, sounds like: "I think that 'I think.'" This is why, as we have said several times, the thinking I seems to precede itself, and appears unattainable, ineffable. This is why the subject of self-reflection appears to be sinking in an abyssal interiority, characterized by the monotonous velocity of infinite regression. But this is a wrong impression. The foundation of self-consciousness is not the descriptive enunciation "I think," but the performative "I speak." This kind of self-reference profits from a heterogeneous element: the thing we do with words, the external, phenomenal, sensible event determined by the enunciation. By referring to itself as *res* (and not as dictum), "I speak" avoids infinite regression. Rather than casting a new meta-I for every episode of the soap opera of introspection, the subject apprehends completely its own way of being in the unity/difference of discourse and action. This unity/difference (or tauto-heterology) becomes manifest in a linguistic action that to a certain extent is always external to the subject, inscribed among the facts of the world. In the end, the foundation of self-consciousness is the circularity of language and praxis, their essential synonymous nature, the becoming unequal of the equal, and the becoming equal of the unequal. In the performative enunciation "I think," the subject recognizes itself as a subject capable of meaning and as a body capable of acting: a "linguistic" as well as "political" animal.

7. A rejection of idealism

Let us summarize our argument. The preconditions for an alienated experience don't have the distinctive relevance of external *res*; rather, they become ungraspable and tyrannical presuppositions. A Word that does not become flesh is alienating. The reification of human nature remedies the privations and the misery of an introverted life.

It does not threaten the transcendental dimension, on the very contrary: it regards it so highly that he frees it from the miserable hegemony of consciousness. The transcendental is the "between" of the human relation, that is, the original public nature of our mind. But this "between," without losing any of its most relevant prerogatives, shows itself in an array of sensible things and facts: the transitional phenomena studied by Winnicott, the technical objects where the pre-individual components of the subject are manifested, the lexical and syntactic texture pre-dating the formation of the singular I. Equally transcendental are the linguistic and acting faculties, which are the foundations of pure consciousness. But these faculties, while maintaining their a priori status, are always incarnated in transient linguistic acts, which are loud and audible. Reification places the transcendental outside the I and by doing so allows it to experience itself directly, preventing it from falling into a state of alienation eternally fluctuating between melancholic asceticism and ironic disenchantment.

The worst flaw of fetishism is not an impulsive recognition of the objectual nature of the preconditions of experience, but, inversely, in their non-recognition. Fetishism is content with attributing an undue spiritual halo to a being or a fact depending on them. The "simple object" theorized by Russell, the reversal of the relation between producers and merchandises, the paralogistic I-substance beloved by metaphysical psychology: these are all examples of a failed, or even parodic, reification. A critique of fetishism consists in indicating with precision what the Flesh of a certain Word is, so that an arbitrary, idolatrous substitution of an insignificant body for the Word becomes impossible. We have seen many times that the cult of interiority doesn't eliminate, but rather justifies and encourages fetishism: if the Word does not become flesh, remaining an invisible presupposition, its superstitious avatars proliferate wildly. If the I-word does not exhibit its own specific objectuality, it is fatally replaced by the Frankenstein of the I-substance. A philosophy pretending to reduce the subject to self-consciousness, incapable of recognizing its external, objectual components, is bound to fluctuate between infinite regression and the devotion to some enigmatic and mocking Odradek.

We don't need to fear or to wish for the realization of reification. Like the erect position and verbal thought, this is a fundamental aspect of the human animal. We need to rectify, at least in part, what we have said at the beginning about its processual, dynamic character. The foundations of subjectivity don't become things in the course of time: they are such from the very beginning. They don't manifest themselves progressively as empirical phenomena: they are always visible. The constitution of the self-reflexive I doesn't percolate, little by little, through new openings, in the world of appearances: it is always already there. Alienation and fetishism are derived possibilities that articulate negatively our reified way of being in historical and social terms. Alienation is a negative possibility; fetishism is a distortion. The socio-historical ways of life (and of course their theoretical representations) that hide or deface the essential objectuality of human nature are either alienated or fetishistic. Reification is an ontological condition that can manifest itself as such or, inversely, can assume the faulty disguise of alienation and fetishism. In this respect, the genuine expressions of reification have a historical and contingent character. For all that concerns its own *parousia*, or revelation, this essential way of being is subject to the aleatory outcomes of social and political controversies. A good example could be the contemporary alternative that faces human relations: a fetishism of merchandises or a salutary, transindividual reification.

In the chapter of *Critique of Pure Reason* called *Refutation of Idealism*, Kant affirms that "even our inner experience, which Descartes considers as undoubted, is possible only on the supposition of outer experience."[23] Our psychological vicissitudes, which are generally considered primordial and certain, are in fact dependent on the reality of the material world that sometimes has seemed problematic and in need of proof. If there were no external objects, persisting independently from various representations, nothing could anchor the Heraclitean flow of my mental activity. What I feel and think is a pure temporal succession, a continuous change that in order to coalesce in an autobiographical narrative needs a permanent background. But this "however, cannot be something within me […] The determination of my existence in time is, consequently, possible only through the existence of actual things, which I perceive outside me."[24] For Kant, interiority is only a reflection, or a consequence, of our interaction with the beings and objects of the world. This is a true "allegiance to things" (in the admirable words of the French poet Francis Ponge),[25] aimed at preventing that the soul's monologues become meaningless and fragmented mutterings. From this reversal of the usual hierarchy between objectual reality and the intimate thoughts of the I we can derive a fundamental principle of reification. However, we will have to radicalize the refutation of idealism well beyond Kant's intention.

On the basis of the arguments proposed in this chapter, but following the direction of Kant's text, we should say that even the determination of pure consciousness (and not only the fluctuating psychological life of an empirical I) is impossible without the perception of external *res*—or rather, without the perception of the external *res* (circumstances, events, actions) that realize the faculties of the human animal, the presuppositions for experience, the relation of the subject to itself. The decisive point is not the necessity of a stable objective world so that we can know what occurs chaotically *in interiore hominis*, but the worldly, that is, exterior to consciousness, location of the very preconditions of subjectivity. A transitional object, just as the action of saying out loud "I speak," are the transcendental *res* that allow us to experience what concerns us the most, that is, the essential characteristics of human nature. What happens when the I perceives these transcendental *res*? When it recognizes in certain external phenomena the exhibition of its very way of being? What happens, finally, when we grasp the perceivable and unperceivable things that manifest what is apparently most hidden, such as the pre-individual residues of a person or the creation of self-consciousness? We have, then, a surprising circularity between the knowing mind and the known object, the facts learned and grasped by the mind. Furthermore, in these cases we can truly speak of a coincidence between the designating I and the designated object. From a cognitive point of view, reification finds its most complete realization in a *tautology* that is neither empty nor trivial, but actually extremely educational.

The late Schelling, wanting to emphasize the paradoxical empiricist vocation of the theological concept of revelation, commented on the phrase from John's Gospel about the Word becoming flesh, contingent phenomenon and perceptible voice saying that for the human being, the ultimate goal can only be that the totality of our inner world be exposed as externally visible to the external world.[26] But this is also, we should now add, the "ultimate goal" of a duly radicalized refutation of idealism.

Part 3

From the Beginning and Right Now

The linguistic faculty can be distinguished from the languages.

— Ferdinand de Saussure

Man is the undefined animal; somehow it is not constituted once for all.

— Arnold Gehlen

History is the true natural history of man.

— Karl Marx

6

Natural History

1. Oxymoron's virtues

The concept of *natural history* may still become the angular stone of a strong and effective materialism. We need, however, to free both the name and the adjective from their metaphorical residue.

By *history*, we mean the contingency of social systems and the changing modes of production, not continental erosion or the evolution of the species. We are not dealing simply with temporal irreversibility, which is the common seal of all entropic processes of energy dispersion *and* of modern proletarian rebellions, but all that separates the latter from the former. Naturalist historians are not charmed by the demon of analogy. They circumscribe sparingly, and discriminate attentively. They care only about the events that can only be deciphered through an analysis of verbal language, of labor, of political praxis. The focus of "natural history" is limited, therefore, to the history of human forms of life, whose only terrain are ethical habits, technologies, class struggles, and changing entanglements of memories and expectations. If we expanded the concept of historicity to include the myriad of unique, unrepeatable, unnecessary and even casual events crowding the annals of geology and biology, we would acquire a panoramic view not that different from the one that we might have on Judgment Day: all phenomena, in fact, would be unified under the sole requirement of *caducity*. This is the only currency allowing us to equate and exchange the most dissimilar things. Nature, which is transient and mortal because it is traversed by the arrow of time, takes on the aspect of a historical drama, while archived historical facts assume the rigidity of fossils. Walter Benjamin showed how the double caducity of the planet and of social organisms fed into the repertoire of baroque allegories.[1] But the first task of natural history is, precisely, to resist the seduction of rhetorical tropes and quickly attain a sober literality.

By natural, we mean the physiological and biological constitution of our species, the innate dispositions that characterize it phylogenetically (starting, of course, with the linguistic faculty), are not dependent at all from different cultural constellations and remain almost the same in the course of time. The adjective has nothing to do with the dubious notion of "second nature" used by contemporary cognitive science to depict (and sometimes to exorcise) the peculiarity of social systems. This notion, used in passing by Marx and then by Lukàcs in *Theory of the Novel*, initially had a polemical, even sarcastic function. By talking about a "second nature," these authors were in fact exposing the pretense of capitalism to constitute a non-historical social organization strictly tied to inevitable anthropological inclinations, and therefore always already valid. Critical thought made fun of this naturalism for managers, refuting the analogy between bourgeois habits and the laws of gravity. The fact that today the image of a "second nature" would still be taken seriously and actually greatly respected is a sad statement about the current status of critical thought. But let us go back to our argument. The nature of "natural history" is only and specifically a *first* nature. It is not an attempt at making the form of the commodity a chemical property of objects, but the unchanging biological core that characterizes the existence of the human animal in the most diverse social-economical formations. Even for the adjective "natural" we need to use a strong protection against metaphorical slippages.

The expression "natural history" is interesting only if the terms constituting it remain in perpetual tension. All hasty reconciliation of these two heterogeneous polarities would disperse the energy of the concept. In fact, we need to bring the heterogeneity to its limit, and to try and connect the antipodes *as such*. What really counts is the immediate relation between the distinctive traits of the *Homo sapiens* as species and the most fleeting cultural dispositions, the biological "always already" of biology and the social "right now," the innate disposition for language and a political decision dictated by exceptional circumstances. Neither metaphorical, nor allegorical, the expression "natural history" might share the virtues of the oxymoron: that is, it postulates an electric spark resulting from the connection of two clearly contrasting elements. In this regard, the criteria cited by Theodor Adorno in a 1932 conference seem to be perspicuous:

> If the question of the relation of nature and history is to be seriously posed, then it only offers any chance of solution if it is possible *to comprehend historical being in its most extreme historical determinacy, where it is most historical, as natural being, or if it were possible to comprehend nature as an historical being where it seems to rest most deeply in itself as nature.*[2]

The possibility of natural history hinges on two conditions: one is natural, the other historical. The first one implies that human nature, which in itself is unchanging, does allow for a maximum of variations in experience and praxis, since otherwise there would be no history. The second one implies that the historical variations sometimes concern themselves with the biological invariants and show them as concrete states of affairs, since otherwise nothing would be "natural." The last sentence is decisive, because it is both necessary and sufficient, and it offers us the thread enabling us to define, although still in abstract terms, the concept-oxymoron at the center of this discussion. Naturalist historiography focuses on the social and political events that confront the human animal with *metahistory*, that is, with the inalterable traits of his species. This kind of historiography collects empirical facts (linguistic, economic, and so forth) that, within a unique cultural conjuncture, manifest what repeats itself since the age of Cro-Magnon. For instance, it collects historically circumscribed discursive forms (such as glossolalia in early Christianity) whose only task is to showcase the linguistic function as a metahistorical prerogative of *Homo sapiens*. I call natural the history that finds in human nature not only its hidden presupposition, but also its manifest content. Historic-natural phenomena reveal the biological invariant, investing it for a moment with a great social and political prominence. Natural history is reflexive: it collects the various occasions when, in the course of time, human praxis focuses on the very requisites that make praxis human; when the *anthropos*, working and talking, relives the most important stages of *anthropogenesis*; when we experience the transcendental conditions of experience. We should add immediately that this reflexivity does not pertain to consciousness, but to the objective structure of historic-natural phenomena.

Marx wrote that history is the true natural history of humanity. This statement is unquestionable, with the condition that we grasp, in the historical sequence, also and maybe especially the *moving* articulation of eternity and contingency, of biology and politics, of repetition and difference. Rather than dissolving the eternal (the distinctive traits of the human species) into the contingent (productive systems, cultural paradigms and so forth) or even worse, reducing the contingent to the eternal, natural history chronicles meticulously their ever changing intersection.

If we want to test the explicatory power of a historic-naturalist approach we need to embark on a difficult journey. Our first step will be the critical analysis of the discussion between Noam Chomsky and Michel Foucault about the notion of "human nature." That dialogue, already so remote from a temporal point of view, documents an essential bifurcation, whose consequences still haunt us today. We need to free ourselves from this hypnotizing event through the elaboration of a position equally distant from those of the two rivals. The issue of "human nature," in itself difficult and pretentious, can find a sober *experimentum crucis* in our understanding of the linguistic function and of its relation with historical languages. After these considerations, we will ask how we can explain *naturalistically* the recurrent opposition between "nature" and "culture," but also what are the socio-historical conditions for the suturing of this break. Only at this point will we be able to go back to our original theme, giving a more concrete definition of the concept of natural history.

2. Foucault and Chomsky on "human nature"

In Eindhoven, in 1971, Chomsky and Foucault had the opportunity to meet face to face for a television program. This was their first and last encounter. The debate circled around the concept of "human nature," that is, on the stable, species-specific basis against which the mercurial variability of historical vicissitudes needs to articulate itself. Chomsky, given his studies on a universal grammar, believes in this basis, and indicates its main characters. Foucault assumes a contrarian position: he differentiates, specifies, objects. The two arguments don't really come into conflict: there is no attrition between them. The duelers often and gladly misunderstand each other, or at least they avoid each other and proceed on parallel lines. Things change in the second part of the conversation, when political and social consequences are derived from the previous considerations on "human nature." At that point, the antagonism between Chomsky and Foucault becomes lively and detailed. We should say right away that the two intellectuals agree on many concrete political objectives (the opposition to the Vietnam War, the unconditional support to the most radical demands of the workers and so forth). The disagreement consists on a question of principle: the possibility of deriving the model for a just society from certain biological prerogatives of the human animal.

The discussion of Eindhoven vividly ratifies the break between naturalist and historical materialism (in the larger, or at least the least compromised, meaning of the terms) that marked the second half of the 20th century and whose consequences are still felt among us. Since 1971, the separation between these two orientations has been complete and inflexible. Any pointed inquiry into production processes and changing power relations has denied itself the possibility to move from acquired to innate characteristics. The paradoxical result has been the inability to see how the latter, that is, the biological invariant, has been managed by contemporary forms of production and power in historically determined ways. On the other hand, the program for a naturalization of the mind and language proposed by Chomsky and then systematically developed by the cognitive sciences has proven to be lacking any historical openings. Cognitive scientists concern themselves with society and politics only outside of their philosophical activity, that is, when they stop thinking. Eindhoven saw the last important attempt at keeping history and biology together as well as its theatrical failure. Both the attempt and the failure revolve around the figure of Chomsky. Differently from his cautious and skeptical followers, he has devoted a large part of his intellectual energies to political activism. This is why he doesn't resign himself easily to the separation between linguistic and social analysis. If elsewhere he limits himself to alternate among the two in a regime of full equality, in Eindhoven he did try to find an intrinsic nexus between the two. He tried, but of course he did not succeed.

Let's examine some crucial parts of the discussion. In order to defend the idea that there is an invariable, that is, metahistorical, human nature, Chomsky calls to the stand as his main witness the linguistic faculty. This faculty belongs to the species, is common to all of its members and is essentially unique with respect to the other species. Linguistic competency is innate: it does not depend from our social environment except from its occasional performances. From the very beginning, our way of using words reveals an "instinctive regularity," that is, a syntactic organization that surpasses by far the partial and often mediocre "data" offered by actual speakers. Like a self-developing organ, language is endowed with selective structures and combinatory schemas whose autonomous productivity are independent from the speaker's empirical experience. Universal grammar, underlying the various historical languages, is part of our genetic patrimony:

> If we were able to specify in terms of, let's say, neural networks the properties of human cognitive structures that make it possible for the child to acquire these complicated systems then I at least would have no hesitation in describing these properties as being a constitutive element of human nature. That is, there is something biologically given, a foundation for whatever we do with our mental capacities in this case.[3]

Foucault's reply is conciliatory in appearance. If he hesitates to embrace the notion of human nature, and actually doesn't trust it much, it is only because he thinks that the general tendency to treat it as a scientific concept is wrong. Looking at it more closely, this notion only has the function of circumscribing a field of research and to separate it carefully from contiguous or rival fields. It is not an object of study, but an epistemological criterion that can be used to determine the limits and the modalities of our inquiries:

> It was not by studying human nature that linguists discovered the laws of consonant mutation, or Freud the principles of the analysis of dreams, or cultural anthropologists the structure of myth. In the history of knowledge, the notion of human nature seems to me to have played the role of an epistemological indicator to designate certain types of discourses in relation to or in opposition to theology or biology or history. I would find it difficult to see in this a scientific concept.[4]

When Chomsky insists on another fundamental aspect of the linguistic faculty (or of human nature, which amounts to the same) it becomes clear that what is at stake is more than a simple methodological nuance. Besides being innate, the linguistic faculty is creative. Each speaker makes "an infinite use of finite means": his or her enunciations, which are derived neither from internal nor internal conditions, tend toward innovation and even unpredictability. Clearly, we are not talking about an exceptional talent, like the one of a theoretical physicist or of a poet, but of a "low rate," normal, diffuse, almost inevitable creativity, which has a biological foundation as well. Neglected by Skinner's behaviorism but also by Saussure's linguistics, the innovative aspect of linguistic performances is strictly related to an original limitation: far from contradicting their power, creativity takes advantage of the structures and schemes that discriminate *a priori* between what can and cannot be said. The uncontested rules of universal grammar and the freedom of linguistic usage depend on each other. This is when Foucault sets diplomacy aside and openly declares his disagreement. It is true that creativity can only arise from a system of binding rules. But Chomsky is wrong in locating these normative principles in the individual mind. The schemes and structures founding all creative variation don't originate in the person. For Foucault, this means that they originate in history. The rules followed by the individual, and from which he can occasionally deviate, are not innate, but are born out of economic, social and political practices.[5] Only those who mistake human nature for a scientific concept instead of an "epistemological indicator" don't acknowledge this basic fact. Because of this initial quid pro quo, the socio-historical vicissitudes of the species are reduced to the psychological structures of the individual. Chomsky holds on and stubbornly defends both the meta-historical nature and the individual aspect of linguistic creativity: "the nature of human intelligence has not changed in any substantial way, at least since the seventeenth century, or probably since Cro-Magnon."[6]

Now we turn our attention on the dispute about "civil disobedience" that ends the Eindhoven conversation. Chomsky doesn't hesitate to deduce a fully developed political engagement from some persistent aspects of human nature. The creativity of language, which is a biological trait of our species, has to be defended through a full blown struggle against all those forms of power (capitalism, centralized state and so on) that are intent at inhibiting or repressing it. If we think that "a fundamental element of human nature is the need for creative work, for creative inquiry, for free creation without the arbitrary limiting effect of coercive institutions, then, of course, it will follow that a decent society should maximize the possibilities for this fundamental human characteristic to be realized."[7] This is how a meta-historical attribute of *Homo sapiens* becomes the pillar of an anarchist-corporatist political position and the criterion for deciding if and when we should disobey the law. The protection of our species-specific creativity is the only principle that can legitimize civil disobedience. While admirable in many ways, this attempt to create an intersection between biology and historical praxis is inconsistent and even dangerous: a scientist emphasizing another aspect of human nature, like, for instance, the need for security, could support just as credibly authoritarian and threatening regimes. It is easy for Foucault (who for once adopts a fully Marxist position) to denounce the contradictions implicit in the proposal of an ideal social model:

> These notions of human nature, of justice, of the realization of the essence of human beings re all notions and concepts which have been formed within our civilization, within our type of knowledge and our form of philosophy, and that as a result form part of our class system; and one can't, however regrettable that

> may be, put forward these notions to describe or justify a fight which should—and shall in principle—overthrow the very fundaments of our society.[8]

Civil disobedience cannot claim to derive from an eternal biological principle, since its objectives only appear during a specific historical conjuncture. "Rather than thinking of the social struggle in terms of justice, one has to emphasize justice in terms of social struggle."[9]

The dispute of Eindhoven caused a malaise whose persistence has become educational. This is its main virtue. When we read its transcription, we feel *doubly unsatisfied.* Our reservations with respect to some of Chomsky's assertions do not translate into an agreement with Foucault's objections, and vice versa: the gaps in Foucault's arguments are not filled by Chomsky's rebuttals. We have to resign ourselves to a permanent state of indecision similar to the one encountered by a person who has to decide about the truthfulness of the sentence "I am lying." Obviously, the readers who fervently support either Foucault or Chomsky are not undecided at all (just as there are people who stubbornly continue to argue about the falsity or the veracity of the enunciation "I am lying"). Chomsky's supporters affirm that the 1971 conversation inaugurates the decline of a historical relativism guilty of dissolving human nature, just like an aspirin tablet, in a kaleidoscope of cultural differences. Foucault's followers, instead, think that Eindhoven saw the defeat of the last of many attempts—at once pretentious and naïve—to promote the myth of a natural reality immune to the density of historical experience. But instead of a true discussion, this is a way of avoiding the adversary: this is just what Chomsky and Foucault did forty years ago. Rather than reproducing the moves of the original confrontation, we should get ready to dwell in the malaise and indecision mentioned above. We need to insist on the simultaneous insufficiency of the two contrasting positions. The "neither … nor" delimits an empty space deserving exploration, and defines precisely enough the field of *natural history*.

Foucault is absolutely right to signal the plausibility of the socio-political hypothesis with regard to all discourse on human nature. But he is wrong when he uses it to deny the existence of human nature. This is a classic case of excessive, overzealous inference. The fact that phylogenetic meta-history is the object of multiple, historically conditioned and fully contingent representations doesn't imply its own disintegration as meta-history. In other words, it doesn't prevent the persistence of certain species-specific characteristics from Cro-Magnon onwards. It is true the biological invariant cannot be separated from a changing historical development, but this is not enough to negate the invariant itself, or to neglect its different modes of appearance—as invariant—on the surface of different social and productive systems. In the last analysis, those who believe in the possibility of a natural history remain unsatisfied by Foucault's arguments because he considers that the recursive appearance of the invariant in different historical circumstances in fact only proves its variability (that is, it becomes the negation of the invariant).

Furthermore, it is impossible to deny Foucault's affirmation that human nature, rather than being an object of inquiry, has often served as a simple "epistemological indicator," a conceptual scheme pre-organizing the scientist's gaze. But if we don't want to fall into the most unbridled transcendental idealism, we need to recognize that the existence of a priori categories (also called schemata or epistemological indicators) is grounded in a species-specific empirical reality: the innate language faculty, the structures of verbal thought and so on. Human nature fully coincides with the empirical reality that stands behind all "epistemological indicators," and therefore does not differ from the material conditions underlying the formation of a priori categories. Foucault says:

> Perhaps the point of difference between Mr. Chomsky and myself is that when he speaks of science he probably thinks about the formal organization of knowledge, whereas I am speaking of knowledge itself, that is to say, I think of the content of various knowledges which is dispersed into a particular society, permeates through that society, and asserts itself as the foundation of its education, for theories, for practices, etc.[10]

Right. But the game is played precisely and exclusively on the "formal organization of knowledge." If we stick to the "content of various knowledges," it is easy to doubt of the existence of meta-historical invariables. Easy, but irrelevant.

We are not satisfied with Chomsky's positions in the Eindhoven discussion for a simple reason: he absorbs the variable in the invariable, he reduces history to meta-history. We could use more cautious and nuanced terms, but this is the heart of the matter. We cannot be distracted by Chomsky's very real political passion. For Chomsky, "a decent society" needs a naturalistic correction of the distortions produced by the vagaries of history. As we have seen, the creativity of language (and therefore of work and scientific research) is an inborn character of *Homo sapiens*, and we have to constantly reaffirm it against the demands of different power structures, which are unjust because they are *un-natural*. Deducing a sociopolitical ideal from a biological invariant allows us to exorcize social and political variations, or at least to limit their bad effects. For Chomsky, an equitable social organization would not be different from a meta-history, and would coincide with the distinctive traits of the human animal, which have remained unchanged since Cro Magnon. Faced with this Rousseauian fantasy, we can't simply say that we should only take into consideration Chomsky's linguistic research and not his political reflections. This strategy is good in an academic setting, but it doesn't do justice to Chomsky's life and work. The shakiness of the nexus that he draws between linguistic faculty and political action does not discredit his politics, but simply his way of conceiving the linguistic faculty (and therefore, human nature). This is the real question: which aspects of Chomsky's linguistics prevent him from articulating a credible relation between the innate and the acquired, the variable and the invariable, the meta-historical and the historical? Which aspects of his theory are incompatible with a naturalist historiography?

There are two fundamental issues. The first one is the following: if we assign a defined (although universal) grammar to the linguistic faculty, that is, a set of rules and schemes, it will end up resembling a historical language, or at least, a derived "average" historical language, losing its status as undetermined potentiality and physiological disposition of the species to verbal articulation. This slip carries truly fatal consequences. If it is reduced to the least common denominator of the historical languages, the linguistic faculty incorporates several historical characters. This has the double disadvantage of undermining meta-history while freezing historical change. The weakening of the distinction between "always already" and "right now" prevails in a hybrid space where biology establishes the criteria for social justice. In order to re-establish the distinction and to distinguish what belongs to each field, we need to abandon the idea that human nature consists of the "creativity of linguistic uses," or in other properties, isolated as little nuggets endowed with their own specific weight. The linguistic faculty guarantees *the historicity* of the human animal, that is, the preconditions of history, but can't found any political or social model. We will come back to this issue.

The second question is that Chomsky and cognitive science create a dangerous relation between the species and the individual. In fact, they have no hesitation in conflating the two without residue. From this point of view they are very Christian, whether they know it or not. "The pagans understood the individual as a part different from the whole of the species, while the Christians believed it to form an immediate, indistinguishable unity with it. [...] For the Christians, God is the idea of the species as an individual."[11] The mistake, of course, does not reside in taking an individual linguistic mind as representative of the species, but in denying or removing *its transindividual character*. Let's be careful: we call "transindividual" not the set of specifications shared by all individuals, but only what pertains to *the relation between* individuals, without belonging to any of them in particular. Transindividuality is what articulates, within one single mind, the difference between the species and the individual. It is an empty, potential space, and not a set of positive properties which, far from being an "in-between," would be the exclusive property of a certain I. In the individual, the transindividual aspects of the linguistic faculty necessarily appear as an *incompletion*, a gap, a potentiality. These defective, but innate, aspects tell us that *the life of the mind is public* from the very beginning. Having neglected the transindividual dimension, Chomsky and the cognitive scientists think that the individual mind is self-sufficient and therefore non-political. According to their script, social praxis only intervenes in the second act of the play, when self-sufficient, essentially private minds start to interact. The public sphere is an option that we could always forego. The "linguistic animal" is not, as such, a "political" one. The noise of history does not grow roots in human nature, on the contrary: it is the latter that is tasked with softening that noise and alleviating its dissonances.

3. Biological invariants and the horizon of religion

Natural history proposes to assess the different forms taken by the biological characteristics of our species on the empirical plane, as they incarnate themselves in fully contingent socio-political phenomena. In particular, it focuses on how the phylogenetic conditions guaranteeing the historicity of the human animal can sometimes take the semblance of *specific historical facts*. It defends, therefore, both the invariability of the invariable and the variability of the variable, excluding all apparently wise compromise. In order to present its claims, natural history has to reject not only the opposite but symmetrical orientations that came to a head in 1971, but also and most of all the alternative that they present: either we dissolve meta-history into empirical history (Foucault), or we fold history into metahistory (Chomsky). Until our choice will be restricted to these two possibilities, natural history will remain an illegal immigrant with no right to citizenship.

Dealing with Chomsky and Foucault is a far more complicated affair. Here we are only addressing their confrontation in Eindhoven, as a symptom of a paralysis that still endures. We wanted to stylize and emphasize a theoretical problem. But this stylization requires an additional step, which no longer concerns those two intellectuals. We are now faced with a radical *aut-aut*: the dissolution of meta-history into history, or the folding of history into metahistory. Strange as it might seem, both options keep a considerable relation with a mythical-religious perspective. The relation is different in the two cases, but equally robust.

The historicist dissolution of meta-history expiates its sins in the reawakening of myth and of religious dispositions. The pretense of reducing the distinctive traits of the species Homo sapiens to production or power relations causes liturgy, or in any case a culture dominated by theological impulses, to take charge of the biological invariant. First nature, once constricted in the Lilliputian swaddles of the so-called "second nature," finds an indirect expression and a mocking reward in the proliferation of values proudly affirming their independence from social and political praxis. Historical materialism, devouring or annihilating natural materialism, shoots itself in the foot: it encourages the apparent de-historicizing of life forms and the reissuing of the sacred on a mass scale. Sebastiano Timpanaro has spoken several times about the vindictive transformation of biological meta-history into religious feelings: "Generally, I believe that we can observe how the non-recognition of man's biological nature brings about a spiritualist reaction, because we are forced to attribute to the 'spirit' all that cannot be explained in socio-economical terms."[12] We could say, ironically, that the true intersection between nature and culture is often insured by the most abstract forms of culture, starting with theology. Religion, since in its own way it underscores the importance of meta-history in socio-political vicissitudes, is the negative image, or the watered-down double, of natural history. In other words, it signals its lack. It is completely wrong to think, as it has happened to bad Marxists, that religion is destined to disappear in a historical context that has overcome economic alienation. Only the historic-naturalist reframing of transcendence, not its negation, can confer a logical dimension to atheism. What lies beyond historical praxis, that is, what is independent from it and always exceeds it, also stands before it: organic and inorganic matter, chemical synapses, physiological constitution and innate dispositions of the human animal. Atheism ceases to be a parasitical and subaltern instance when it articulates differently the relation between biological meta-history and social history, between the invariant and the variable, "always already" and "right now." It certainly can't do so if it retreats into the second term of these oppositions omitting or mocking the first.

Let us consider the other possibility presented by the *aut-aut*: folding historical change into an array of eternal meta-historical determinations. In this case, religion is no longer a punitive penance, but actually becomes an operational *model*. Ernesto de Martino—like Mircea Eliade or Gerardus van der Leeuw—characterizes the mythic-religious procedures very concisely: "Ritual is a behavior that always brings the historical 'once' to a meta-historical one, that is also 'once and forever.' [...] History is resolved into an identical meta-history that repeats itself."[13] The uncanny metastasis of becoming is exorcised with an evocation of what stays the same and repeats itself without interruptions since the very beginning: *ab illo tempore*, say liturgical formula, or "since Cro-Magnon" in Chomsky's words. The uncertainty threatening those who have to deal with contingent and unforeseeable events can be subdued rarefying the web of history (it doesn't matter whether we use epistemological or ritual expedients) so that we can connect the present to the beginning of everything (the creation of the cosmos, the phylogenetic attributes of *Homo sapiens* or anything else.) Today's endeavors find their value and legitimacy in the enduring relation with a mythic past, that is, with an anterior situation determining the invariance of the archetype. Thus, a politics that wants to defend the innate creativity of linguistic use from any power relation, ends up brandishing an immutable presupposition against all situations that appear to deny it. This kind of politics, directly deduced from certain prerogatives of the human animal is a "return technique that goes back to a bad past and attenuates the historicity of becoming."[14] More cautious, and more importantly, less generous than Chomsky, his cognitivist disciples have renounced this kind of deduction, severing all residual relation between biological meta-history and political praxis. Still, there is no difference whatsoever between the impassionate attempt to conceive the contingent "once" in relation to the species-specific "once for all" and the simple expulsion of the "once" from the horizon of research. As a whole, cognitivist *ideology* has played a role similar to mythic-religious thought (which has also served as an authoritative administrator of human nature): the recourse to the biological archetype has often been a mean to dispel the fears caused by the paradoxes inherent to socio-political events.

4. The linguistic faculty

Natural history finds its true testing ground in the way it conceives the linguistic faculty. To say it in one breath, I am convinced that the existence of a generic faculty, separate from the myriad historical languages, clearly attests to the non-specialized character of the human animal, that is, to its innate familiarity with a *dynamis*, a potentiality, that can never be fully realized. Instinctual unpreparedness and chronic potentiality: these invariant aspects of human nature, deducible from the linguistic faculty, imply an unlimited variability of production relations and life forms without, however, suggesting any blueprint for a just society. This is what determines the extreme contingency of political praxis, from Cro-Magnon to the present.

Diego Marconi, calling our attention on the Eindhoven discussion, credits Chomsky with having opposed the crucial argument of historicism, which sounds more or less like this: "the diversity of languages attests to the independence of language from biology; but its language is the heart of a culture and the vehicle—if not the essence—of a form of thought. Therefore, what is natural in the human being (in the biological sense of the term) does not determine what is truly human in him, that is, his thought and his culture."[15] Chomsky's confutation, that justifies the renewed credit given to the notion of "human nature," consists, as we know, in underscoring the presence of a species-specific faculty endowed with its own grammatical structures, lying underneath the various historical languages. According to Marconi, the emphasis on the innate linguistic faculty has done away with the theories considering that "humanity, more than a species, was an ability to interpret."[16] But in fact, what is the linguistic faculty? Once we admit without reservations its biological character, the main question is still open: does the faculty coincide perfectly with the ultimate reality of historical languages, or is it simply their precondition? Are we dealing with a well-defined plenitude, or, on the contrary, with a still indeterminate potential? In the following pages, we will try to indicate the most promising line of thought. Naturally, signaling a path is not the same as walking on it. Our necessarily concise discussion will be organized around some peremptory assertions that could be called "theses" only in jest.

a) *What counts the most is the irreducible, even* incommensurable, *difference that exists between the linguistic faculty and the historical languages. Neither of them dominates the relation or undermines the other: the determinant factor is their permanent separation and interconnection.*

By faculty, we mean the innate physical ability to enunciate articulate sounds, that is, the physiological requirements that allow us to produce an enunciation: a mouth emancipated from prehensile tasks thanks to our erect position, lowering of the epiglottis, fleshy and mobile tongue muscle, specific properties of our tracheo-laryngal tract and so forth. By language, we mean, as is customary, a particular phonetic, lexical and grammatical system, whose every part will never be founded on anything else than "the functioning of linguistic oppositions."[17] The struggle for human nature finds the majority of its weaponry in this conceptual couple. We have seen that those who privilege the faculty tend to neglect social and cultural changes, underscoring the existence of an invariant and metahistorical script. On the contrary, those who privilege the historical languages consider that only the latter, and not the inaugural and rarefied faculty, allow us to grasp the true functioning of verbal language and, therefore, the truly distinctive trait of the human animal. The faculty is biological, the different languages are historical; the first is innate, the second is acquired; one pertains to the individual mind while the other is inconceivable outside of a social context. These are the stakes, and the roles are clearly assigned. The linguist concerned with the linguistic faculty will deal with the substantive "nature," the one devoted to the historical languages will delve on the adjective "human." It is obvious that the two duelists, being perfectly polite, won't fail to pay homage to the dominating passion of their adversary, but this is pure *bon ton.*

However, the pair faculty/historical languages, invoked by both parties, quickly shrinks and evaporates. No matter the prevalent perspective, the two concepts don't remain separate. The hiatus that distinguishes them weakens progressively until it disappears. One of the two poles ends up annexing the other, reducing it to its subaltern corollary or feeble premise: in one case, the faculty-prototype already includes, as colorful but inessential additions, the historical languages; in the other, the historical language is the final result of the linguistic faculty, which has then fulfilled its propaedeutic function. We need to elaborate a way of thinking that would make the assimilation of the two antipodes impossible. Those who try to locate the historical languages within the faculty, or the faculty into the historical languages inevitably assume that the container and its content are close and commensurable. But this is not true. Neither convergent nor mutually translatable, the faculty and the historical languages show a persistent heterogeneity, which prevents any kind of reduction *ad unum*.

b) *The linguistic faculty fully coincides with the ancient notion of* dynamis, *or potentiality*.

The linguistic faculty is a potential language or the potentiality for language. Though complementary and even inseparable, action and potential are still extremely heterogeneous terms. We call "act" what is real and present, with a determined content and possessed of unique properties, while "potential" indicates something absent and still undefined. In its original meaning, *dynamis* is synonymous with *me einai*: non being, lack, emptiness. Only the animal that is born aphasic has a linguistic faculty. Or rather: only the animal who lacks a repertoire or signals biunivocally related to the various hostile or hospitable configurations of the surrounding environment.

Saussure thought that the linguistic faculty was separate from historical languages but could not operate without them, and furthermore that parole, or individual speech "is necessary for the establishment of language, and historically its actuality always comes first."[18] The separation between faculty and historical languages cannot be bridged because the faculty can't manifest itself independently. If it had its own reality, with articulated structures and specific performances, the linguistic faculty would be an ancestral or archetypal language (a universal Sanskrit, so to speak), so that it would differ from the historical languages only by extension or degree, as it occurs for a class and its sub-classes. But the faculty itself is inactual, amorphous, lacking positive determinations. Potentiality is a whole without parts, indivisible in quotas and percentages. It relates to its corresponding acts like an irrational number relates to a rational one: in both cases, they are incommensurable.[19]

The linguistic faculty is both biological and potential. It is not a topographically accurate map, but a no-man's land travelled by the infant, the aphasic, the translator.

c) *It is misleading to mistake the linguistic faculty for a protolanguage spoken by the entire species, but so is thinking that it is a mere premise for the mother tongue that would vanish without trace once we have learned it. Far from disappearing, the potential-faculty* co-exists *with the historical language, and characterizes the entire experience of the speaker.*

If we identify the faculty with a given set of specific structures, we are not really dealing with the faculty, but with the minimum common denominator of historical languages. We eliminate the relation aphasia/faculty, wrongly assimilating an empty ability-to-speak to a set of general rules that would govern every utterance. The research concerning a "universal grammar," although fundamental, does not address the faculty itself (at most, it can study its passage into the different languages).

Against the thesis that sees the faculty as a temporary stage, we could cite Saussure when he says that "in dealing with speech, it is completely misleading to assume that the problem of early characteristics differs from the problem of permanent characteristics."[20] The relation between historical languages and linguistic faculty, fullness and emptiness, inactuality and presence is not limited to early childhood, but it keeps seeping through the learned speech of the adult speaker. In other words: in fully developed linguistic praxis, a defective or lacking element always persists. We fully share Franco Lo Piparo's remarks about aphasia as a "permanent linguistic condition" among speakers:

> Since aphasia, or absentia linguae is the point of departure of humanity, the historical languages are the always unfinished result of a progressive and laborious human construction. The mechanism that initiates the psycho-linguistic process is the unresolved tension between a poverty of codes and the necessity to speak and be understood.[21]

The *access* to language is not an inaugural, transient event, but a constant way of experiencing language. Emile Benveniste says that any speaker, when they enunciate an utterance, has to appropriate his or her own language. This is an important remark that we need to take literally. It would be nonsensical to appropriate something that is already ours. The necessity of appropriating alludes to a preliminary condition (*chronic*, and not limited to childhood) of lack and aphasia that we always need to overcome. This condition, marked by a *me einai*, is nothing else that the indeterminate *potentia loquendi*, since before the utterance language is only the possibility of language.

In a way, the linguistic faculty is a generic predisposition, without grammatical schemes and irreducible to a more or less elaborate set of possible enunciations. It is innate but unrefined, biological but purely potential. On the other hand, this predisposition persists as an inalterable background even when we master a certain historical language. The potential is not an accidental gap, destined to be filled. Even if I spoke incessantly for hundreds of years, my linguistic faculty would remain intact in its distinctive traits: indeterminacy, latency and so on. The *dynamis* does not disappear when we actually utter a sentence, nor does it become an archive of predefined executions. The so-called "creativity" of language, that Chomsky mentions several times, is dependent on the permanent crossing of emptiness and fullness, irrational and rational numbers, potentiality and act, and not from a set of actual properties belonging to a super-language undergirding all mother tongues.

d) *The linguistic faculty confirms the instinctual poverty of the human animal, its undefined character and the constant disorientation that defines it.*

The philosophers close to Chomsky think that the linguistic faculty is a highly specialized instinct, but we need to add that this is a specialization in polyvalence and generalization, or an instinct to adopt non-determined behaviors. It is clear that saying that the linguistic animal is supremely capable of foregoing any specific capability amounts to little more than sophistry. Of course, the linguistic faculty is also a biological patrimony. But not all innate faculties function as a detailed and univocal instinct. The ability to speak, although genetic, is only a *dynamis*, a potentiality. And potentialities, strictly speaking, insofar as they are not a set of well-defined hypothetical performances, coincide with a condition of indeterminacy and uncertainty. The linguistic animal is a potential, *non-specialized animal.*

The concept of potentiality sums up and clarifies anew some remarkable biological (Bolk, Portmann, Gould) paleontological (Leroi-

Gourhan) and anthropological (Gehlen, but already Herder) discoveries. Here I will just cite two iconic passages. Leroi-Gourhan writes:

> Had development continued toward ever-increasing corticalization of the neuromotor system, our evolution would have stopped at a stage comparable to that of the most advanced insects. What happened instead was that the motor areas were overtaken by zones of association having a very different character that, instead of orienting the brain toward ever more developed technical specialization, opened up unlimited possibilities of generalization—unlimited at any rate by comparison with the possibilities offered by zoological evolution. Throughout our evolution, ever since the reptiles, the human appears as the inheritor of creatures that escaped anatomical specialization. Neither human teeth nor hand, neither human foot nor, when all is said and done, brain has attained the perfection of the mammoth's teeth, the horse's hand and foot, or the brain of certain birds—with the result that humans have remained capable of just about every possible action.[22]

The lack of specialized instincts characteristic of *Homo sapiens* can be deduced first and foremost from the linguistic faculty. On this point, Herder was very clear:

> That the human being is far inferior to the animals in strength and sureness of instinct, indeed that he quite lacks what in the case of so many animal species we call abilities for and drives to art, is certain.[23]
>
> What language does the human being possess as instinctively as each animal species possesses its language in, and in accordance

> with, its own sphere? The answer is short: none! And precisely this short answer is decisive [...] The bee hums just as it sucks, the bird sings just as it makes a nest. But how does the human being speak by nature? Not at all.—just as he does little or nothing through sheer instinct as an animal. I make an exception in the case of the newborn child of the cry of its sensitive machine—otherwise, this child is dumb.[24]

Potentialities, lack of specialization: the phylogenetic basis of both is neoteny. The incomplete character of the human animal, his constant indecision and his entire innate dynamis are rooted in various manifestations of organic and anatomical primitivism, or, one might also say, of his genetic incompleteness. Homo sapiens is always born prematurely, and this is why he remains an undefined animal. In the words of Eric Lennerberg:

> By extrapolation, we may assume that the maturational events of the chimpanzee brain during childhood differ from those of man in that at birth his brain is probably much more mature and all parameters are probably more stabilized than in man. [...] Pertinent to man's prolonged maturational history is the hypothesis that man constitutes a "fetalized" version of a more generalized primate developmental course.[25]

Neoteny explains not only the instability of our species, but also its related need for uninterrupted learning. To our *chronic infancy* corresponds a *chronic non-adaptation* that has to be constantly alleviated through social and cultural processes. A prolonged infancy coincides with the transindividual component of the human mind, always unrecognized by the cognitive sciences. Let's remember that the transindividual is what pertains solely to the relations among individuals. In the individual, the "among" exists only as a lack or an empty place. This potential, non-saturated space guarantees from the beginning the public nature of the mind, and therefore is the same thing as the "persistence of juvenile traits in adult subjects."

The best confirmation of neoteny can actually be found precisely in the authors that want to question it. For instance, when Konrad Lorenz criticizes Gehlen's hypothesis stating that a whole array of organic insufficiencies forces the human animal to continuously acquire new adaptive techniques, he does remark that many other species, although endowed with an abundance of specialized instincts, need to go through a long apprenticeship phase. Infancy, with its wealth of potentialities and its learning processes, would not be, then, an exclusive characteristic of *Homo sapiens*. Except that, when it is time to conclude, Lorenz himself defends the only really important aspect of the thesis that he is trying to debunk: the irreversibility, or the persistence, of human infancy:

> One thing in particular differentiates the explorative behavior of any animal from the human one: it appears only during a short phase of animal development. All that a raven acquires in the first stage of its life through active experimentation, so similar to the human one, is immediately fixed by exercises that become less and less variable and adaptable, to the point of becoming almost indistinguishable from instinctive behaviors. [...] In the human being, instead, explorative behaviors continue into old age: man is, and remains, a becoming being.[26]

We can understand neoteny and all the other traits typical of our species only if we fully grasp the concept of *dynamis*, or *potentiality*.

The decisive factor is the radical opposition between potentiality (indivisible, rough, persistent) and potential acts (just as determined as real ones in content and form). Non-human animals certainly have at their disposal a repertoire of potential acts, many of which can be learned: the alligator standing on the edge of the water can still swim; the raven and the crow learn a certain number of virtual operations in order to procure food. We define as neotenic, or a chronic infant, only the living being familiar with a permanent and inarticulate dynamis untranslatable in a series of discrete operations (real or virtual as they may be). Neotenic is only the living being that is continuously faced with the *me einai* of inactuality and absence.[27]

Biologically related to neoteny, the potentiality of the human animal corresponds to the lack of a circumscribed and well-articulated habitat where he would insert himself, once for all, thanks to an innate expertise. If, as Gehlen thought, a habitat is defined by the conditions that allow a certain organism to survive thanks to its innate organization, it goes without saying that a non-specialized organism also lacks a habitat. Its perceptions are not harmonically transformed in univocal behaviors, but they cause an overload of undifferentiated stimuli, which are not finalized toward a specific operational task. In a marginal remark, Kafka wrote that non-human animals, although trapped in a specific habitat, seem calm and happy because "they have never been expelled from the garden of Eden." Deprived of an ecological niche extending its body like a prosthesis, the human animal suffers from a permanent state of insecurity even in the absence of specific dangers. We can certainly agree with Chomsky when he says that "the way we grow does not reflect properties of the physical environment, but rather our essential nature."[28] We must add, though, that "our essential nature" is characterized first and foremost by the inexistence of a specific habitat and, therefore, by a lasting disorientation.

The instability of the human animal never disappears completely. This is why our potentialities remain the same, without exhausting itself in certain acts. This is why the linguistic faculty, the aphasic ability to speak, is not resolved in a language, but is present as such in every enunciation. Contrary to what is implied in a familiar but incongruous expression, the act does not realize the potential, but actually is opposed to it.[29] When we perform a particular action or we say something specific, we are setting aside, for a while, our inarticulate *dynamis*, eschewing its inherent uncertainty. This is clearly an antagonistic relation. If our potential is characterized by indeterminacy and homelessness, our actions don't reinforce it, but in fact oppose it and call it into question.

5. The irruption of metahistory in social praxis: state of exception or routine?

We said at the beginning that the main task of natural history consists in collecting the social and political events that put the human animal in direct relation with metahistory, that is, with the unchangeable biological constitution of the species. The maximally contingent phenomena that show the unchanging human nature in different ways but with the same immediacy can be considered historic-natural. My previous remarks on the linguistic faculty allow us to define with greater precision the meta-historical constants on which historical praxis intervenes in a circular or reflexive manner. The biological invariant characterizing the human animal since Cro-Magnon is a *dynamis*, or a potentiality: it is a lack of specialization, neoteny, and the absence of a univocal *habitat*. The questions confronting natural history are the following: which sociopolitical circumstances expose the lack of biological specialization typical of *Homo sapiens*? When and how does the generic ability-to-speak, different from the historical languages, assume a fundamental role within a certain mode of production? Under which economic or ethical guises does neoteny become visible?

In traditional societies, including—to a certain extent—classic industrial ones, inarticulate potentials gain the visibility of an empirical state of affairs only in emergency situations, that is, during a crisis. In ordinary situations, instead, the species-specific biological background is hidden, or even questioned, by the organization of work and solid communicative habits. In other words, there is a strong discontinuity, or rather an antinomy, between "nature" and "culture." Those who object that this discontinuity is nothing more than a mediocre cultural convention due to the melancholy anthropocentrism of spiritual philosophers are just trying to make their own lives a bit easier, instead of attending to a far more interesting task: finding the *biological* reasons of the lasting separation between biology and society. Naturalizing the mind and language without giving a naturalist explanation of the antinomy "nature" and "culture" reduces the whole issue to a … clash of ideas, and ends up in the most shameful incoherence.

Let us stick to familiar, even stereotypical formulas. We call "potential" a physical organism deprived of a natural habitat, constantly adapting to an eternally indeterminate vital context—that is, to a *world* where the abundance of perceptive stimuli doesn't easily become an effective operational code. The world is not a particularly vast and varied habitat, nor the class of all possible habitats. On the contrary: we have a world *only* when there isn't any habitat. Social and political praxis creates a temporary remedy for this absence (in different and contrasting ways), building *pseudo-habitats* where indiscriminate and multi-directional stimuli are selected in order to promote useful behaviors. This praxis, therefore, is a response to its unchanging meta-historical presupposition. Or, even better, it attests to it precisely in its attempt to correct it. Using a concept coming from Peirce's semiotics, we could say that culture is a "sign by contrast," indicating a species-specific instinctual haplessness: it denotes its object only by virtue of its polemical relation with it. Our vulnerability to the world becomes visible first and foremost as an immunization against the world, thanks to the adoption of repetitive and foreseeable behaviors. Our non-specialization is expressed in a meticulous division of labor, or in a hypertrophic diversity of permanent roles and unilateral tasks. Neoteny expresses itself as the ethico-political defense of neotenic indecision. As biological mechanism aimed at preserving the species, culture needs to stabilize the "indefinite animal," to alleviate or obfuscate its disorientation, reducing its characteristic *dynamis* to a definite repertoire of potential acts. Human nature often implies a contrast between its expressions and its premises.

Over this generalized backdrop, a crucial point becomes visible, rich in nuances and subtleties. We have already talked about it: in traditional societies, the biological invariant (language faculty as distinct from historical languages, rough potentials, non-specialization, neoteny and so forth) acquires an exaggerated historical visibility only when a particular pseudo-habitat is subject to violent transformative pressures. This is why natural history mostly coincides with the *history of a state of exception*. It describes a situation where a form of life is no longer obvious, becoming fragile and problematic. Our cultural defenses become useless and we are forced to go back, for a time, to the "primal scene" of the anthropogenic process. It is in these circumstances that the chronic homelessness of the human animal assumes a contingent *political* relevance.

The collapse of a form of life, accompanied by the irruption of metahistory in the simple repertoire of historical facts, is what Ernesto de Martino—one of the few original Italian philosophers of the 20th century—called a "cultural apocalypse." This is the historically determined situation (economic stress, sudden technological transformation and so forth) that makes visible to the naked eye and renders problematic the difference between linguistic faculty and historical languages, inarticulate potential and well-structured grammars, world and habitat. Among the many symptoms announcing an "apocalypse" according to de Martino, one is of strategic importance for natural history. The undoing of a cultural constellation causes, among other things, "an excess of semanticity irreducible to specific meanings."[30] We are faced with a progressive indeterminacy of speech: it becomes difficult to "bend a possible signifier into a real signified."[31] Speech, deprived of univocal referents, is full of "dark allusions," remaining in the chaotic realm of the ability to speak (an ability to speak greater than any actual elocution). This "excess of semanticity irreducible to specific meanings" is simply the linguistic *faculty*.

During the apocalyptic crisis of a form of life, the innate biological faculty shows fully its constant separation from any historical language. To the preeminence acquired by the fluctuating ability-to-speak corresponds an abnormal fluidity of states of affairs and a growing behavioral indecision. De Martino says that "things don't remain within their familiar limits, and lose their daily use appearing to have lost any memory of possible behaviors."[32] The world, no longer selectively filtered through a system of cultural habits, shows itself as an amorphous and enigmatic context. Thus, the explosion of an ethico-social order reveals two interrelated aspects of "human nature": the linguistic faculty distinct from the historical languages, and a world irreducible to any (pseudo) habitat. This double revelation, however, is temporary and parenthetic. The apocalypse, the state of exception, results in the institution of new cultural niches capable of hiding and attenuating once again the biological invariant, that is, our inarticulate and chaotic *dynamis*.

But this is only true of traditional societies. Contemporary capitalism has radically transformed the relation between unchanging phylogenetic prerogatives and historical praxis. Today's forms of life don't hide the disorientation and the instability of the human animal but, on the very contrary, they push them to their extreme and systematically valorize them. Our amorphous potentiality, that is, the persistence of infantile traits, does not flash ominously during a crisis, but pervades every aspect of the most banal *routine*. Our society of generalized communication is far from fearing an excess of semanticity not resulting in determined meanings, and in fact benefits from it, conferring the utmost importance to the undetermined linguistic faculty. According to Hegel, the main task of philosophy is to think one's own time. This proverbial sentence is a screeching noise for those who indulge in studying the ahistorical mind of the isolated individual, and needs to be updated thus: the preeminent task of philosophy is to come to terms with the unprecedented superposition of eternity and contingency, of the biological invariant and sociopolitical change that is the unique connotation of our time.

Let us be clear: it is because of this superposition that the notion of "human nature" has been enjoying a new prestige in the last few decades. This is not due to astonishing scientific breakthroughs (such as Chomsky's merciless critique of Skinner's *Verbal Behavior*, or other similar instances), but to an array of social, economic and political conditions. Saying otherwise is just another symptom of cultural idealism (mostly of the academic variety) on the part of those scholars who never stop waving the banner of a naturalization of the mind and of language. Human nature finds itself at the center of attention not because we are finally dealing with biology and no longer with history, but because the biological prerogatives of the human animal have acquired an unexpected role in today's productive processes. In other words, this happens because we are witnessing a peculiar empirical manifestation of certain phylogenetic, that is, metahistorical, invariants characterizing *Homo sapiens'* existence. If a *naturalistic* explanation of the autonomy that "culture" maintains in traditional societies is indeed pertinent, so is a *historical* explanation of the essential role that human "nature" has achieved within postfordist capitalism.

Today, natural history finds its object in our everyday existence, not a state of emergency. Rather than reflecting on the end of a cultural constellation, it needs to deal with its full deployment. It doesn't stop at the investigation of "cultural apocalypses," but grasps the totality of current events. Since biological metahistory no longer appears at the limit of life forms, where they crumble hopelessly spinning their wheels, but is situated at their geometrical center signaling their perfect functioning, all social realities can rightly be considered *historico-natural phenomena.*

The lack of specialized instincts and of a strictly defined ecosystem, from Cro-Magnon until today, are now considered remarkable economic assets. It isn't difficult to recognize the clear relation between certain characteristics of "human nature" and the sociological categories most pertinent to the current situation. The biological non-specialization of *Homo sapiens* doesn't remain in the background, but rather acquires the utmost historical visibility as the universal *flexibility* of professional tasks. The only professional talent that really counts in postfordist production is being used to the unusual, that is, the ability to react immediately to the unknown. A univocal competency, modulated in every detail, is now a true handicap for those who have to sell their labor. In addition, neoteny, that is, chronical infancy and the constant need to train oneself, immediately translates itself, without any mediation, in the social rule of continuing education. The weaknesses related to the "premature birth" of the human animal have become productive assets. What we learn is not important (roles, techniques, and so on): what matters is showing the pure ability to learn, which always exceeds its particular actuations. Furthermore, it is obvious that the permanent precariousness of employment, and even more the instability experienced by contemporary migrants, reflect in historically determined ways the original lack of a uniform and predictable *habitat*. Precariousness and nomadism reveal in the social field the incessant and multiple pressures exerted by a *world* that is never an environment. This superabundance of undifferentiated stimuli is not only true in extreme cases, but in our everyday lives. This is not an inconvenience that needs to be corrected, but the vital ground of today's productive processes. And finally, we come to the most important observation: the inarticulate potential that cannot be reduced to a series of predetermined potential acts acquires an extrinsic, even pragmatic aspect in the definition of labor ability. This term designates the different psycho-physical abilities belonging to the human species, taken as still unused *dynamis*. Our labor ability, today, is largely synonymous with our linguistic faculty. And the linguistic faculty, as labor potential, manifests very clearly its difference with respect to grammatically structured historical languages. Linguistic faculty and labor potential are situated on the border between biology and history, except that today this border has acquired specific historical characteristics.

Saying that the linguistic faculty is emblematic of contemporary forms of life, just like neoteny, non-specialization, the lack of habitat, does not mean that they are not regulated. On the contrary. Our familiarity with multiple potentials demands as its inevitable corollary the existence of norms that are infinitely more detailed than those regulating a cultural pseudo-environment. These norms, actually, are so detailed that in fact they only pertain to one single instance, to a single contingent and unreproducible occasion. The flexibility of labor performances implies an unlimited variability of norms, but also, in the short term of their existence, their excessive rigidity. These are ad hoc rules, which describe in detail the way to perform a certain action, and only that one. Just when the linguistic *faculty* acquires its utmost socio-political importance, it ends up appearing, rather ironically, as a system of elementary *signals*, aimed at facing a certain situation. The *excess* of semanticity non-reducible to determined meanings is often reversed, becoming a compulsive recourse to stereotyped formulas and can assume the characteristics, in an apparent paradox, of a *lack* of semanticity. This oscillation is due, in both its polarities, to the absence of stable and articulate pseudo-environments. The world, no longer filtered through a protective cultural niche, is experienced in all of its indeterminacy and potentialities (the excess of semanticity); but this obvious indeterminacy, which needs to be contained and delayed each time anew, causes stilted behaviors, obsessive tics, the drastic impoverishment of our *ars combinatoria* and the inflation of fleeting but ironclad rules (the lack of semanticity). Continuing education and job precariousness, while affording us a full exposition to the world, also encourage its reduction to either a spectral or a mawkish dollhouse.

This explains the surprising connection between the language faculty and monotonous signals.

In traditional societies, then, the biological invariant comes to the fore when a form of life implodes and dissolves, while in contemporary capitalism we perceive it when everything functions regularly. Today, natural history, normally intent at recording with the precision of a seismographer all sorts of crises and states of exception, focuses instead on the ordinary running of the production processes. In our time, the biological characters of Homo sapiens (linguistic faculty, non-specialization, neoteny and so on) perfectly coincide with the most important sociological categories (labor ability, flexibility, continuing education and so on). Adorno's words, quoted earlier as a methodological criterion, have now found their factual realization, since "*historical being in its most extreme historical determinacy, where it is most historical*" is truly, in all of its manifestations, a "natural being" while human nature, just "*where it seems to rest most deeply in itself as nature*," has become a fully "natural being." Two short sentences by Marx taken from his *1844 Manuscripts* can easily describe the current situation. The first one states that "we see how the history of industry and the established objective existence of industry are the open book of man's essential powers, the exposure to the senses of human psychology [...] A psychology for which this, the part of history most contemporary and accessible to sense, remains a closed book, cannot become a genuine, comprehensive and real science."[33] In other words: today's industry—based on neoteny, the linguistic faculty and potentialities—is the extroverted, empirical, pragmatic image of the human psyche, of its invariant and metahistorical characteristics (including the transindividual traits happily ignored by the cognitive sciences). Contemporary industry, therefore, is the only credible manual for a philosophy of the mind. Here is Marx's second sentence, "All history is the preparation for "man" to become the object of sensuous consciousness."[34] If we eliminate the eschatological emphasis (history prepares nothing at all, of course), we can still say that in the age of flexibility and continuing education human nature constitutes a quasi-perceivable evidence and the immediate content of social praxis.

6. Materialism and revelation. For a semiotic of natural-historical phenomena

Now that we are coming to an end, it seems useful to retrace our steps and to redefine with less primitive means the concept of natural history. The road traveled can shed light on our point of departure. The whole building is called upon to strengthen its own supporting walls. In the previous pages, we indicated the preferences and the idiosyncrasies of naturalistic historiography, the roads that it can open or close, its constructive character and its polemical vein. We have also defined its field, listing and evaluating the phenomena that are its object. We still lack, however, a complete picture, and a dispassionate assessment of the influence that the historic-naturalistic position can have with respect to a number of traditional philosophical questions. The following pages, which are to be read as a reiteration and a development of the definitions given in the first section of this chapter, are structured around four related issues and keywords: a) semiotics; b) revelation; c) phenomenon; d) politics.

a) Natural history is a semiotics, for three main reasons: it takes the variable as the sign of the invariable; it denotes the biological through its social name; it recognizes in the contingent a detailed figure of the eternal. However, we still have to elucidate the properties of historic-natural signs, that is, their specific way to *stand in* for their referent. For reasons of brevity, I use the categories elaborated by Peirce. Natural history considers the phenomena it studies as the *icons* (not the *indexes* nor the *symbols*) of a number of metahistorical prerogatives of the human animal.

Let us sketch the portrait of these semiotic notions—which by the way are quite well-known—keeping in mind what is at stake here: what distinguishes the icon from the index is also what separates natural history from other philosophical orientations. Peirce calls "a sign which stands for something merely because it resembles it *an icon*."[35] The icon presents three main attributes: a strict analogy with the denoted object, causal independence from it, and partial irreducibility to mental operations of its user. An index instead is a clue, or sometimes even a consequence, for the thing that it defines. An index for the rain is the barometer recording the low pressure, just as a knock on the door is the index for a visitor. A symbol, instead, is a conventional sign, which "incorporates a habit, and is indispensable to the application of any intellectual habit, at least."[36] Peirce believes that our words are almost all symbols. The word "bird" doesn't resemble at all the object it designates (and therefore it is not an icon), nor does it refer to its presence: if it really designates a certain animal it is only thanks to an autonomous mental process on the part of the "interpreter."

Differently from the index, which is physically related to its referent (quite often as its sufficient cause), the icon has no dynamic relation with the object it represents. Differently from the symbol, the icon is the exclusive result of a mental act, since it denotes its object solely because of its own characteristics.

Certain empirical, historically determined facts, are *icons of human nature*. This means that we can recognize an objective resemblance between these facts and some aspects of such nature. For example, the current flexibility of working tasks denotes the non-specialization of the human animal precisely because it recalls our essential traits (instinctual poverty, indecision, adaptability and so on). Like any true icon, however, flexibility is independent, causally speaking, from the metahistorical referent it resembles: it is not caused by our biological non-specialization, it is simply the contingent and controversial result of today's productive relations. Furthermore, as an icon, flexibility is not a conventional sign and therefore cannot be fully reduced to the mental processes of the historiographer. The mind of the "interpreter" grasps the material affinity between the icon and the object, but it does not institute it. We need to add, for the sake of exhaustiveness, that historical natural phenomena—which can only be analyzed through sociopolitical concepts but still resemble a metahistorical structure—correspond to the two kinds of icon described by Pierce: the image and the diagram. The image is the iconic sign that faithfully reproduces the denoted object by means of its simple qualities (physical aspect, physiognomic traits and so on). The diagram, instead, shares with its referent only the relation among its parts (such as a map or an algebraic equation). The generic labor potential, which is not reducible to a predetermined list of possible tasks, is the historical image of the inarticulate potential that has always characterized the human animal. "Cultural apocalypses," instead, are diagrams, because they show on a smaller scale the relation between chronic disorientation (the "excess of semanticity") and the creation of cultural filters (uniform and predictable behaviors) that is the basis of all human societies.

We should also briefly discuss the nefarious consequences of mistaking social and political history for either the *index* or the *symbol* of the biological invariant. Only this comparison can truly express the philosophical importance of the icon. Let's consider the first error: considering history as the index of metahistory, politics as the symptom of biology, the "right now" as the index of the "always already." Not unlike the knock on the door or the barometer, historical events are considered as the immediate effect of their denoted object (the phylogenetic traits of *Homo sapiens*). The consequence is easily drawn: just as all effects refer back to their causes, so must history-as-index be entirely considered as the effect of metahistory, that is, of all that has endured from Cro-Magnon onwards. As index of human nature, social and political praxis has no autonomy, gaining a diagnosis of epistemological irrelevance. Isn't this the position of the cognitive sciences and, at least in part, of Chomsky in the exchange at Eindhoven? And now for the second mistake: history is the symbol of metahistory. The relation between contingent events and biological presuppositions becomes a purely conventional one, stemming from the mind that uses it. Since the mind of the historiographer is similarly conditioned, the species-specific invariant signified by the symbol is a simple cultural construction, subject to innumerable transformations. Also in this case, the consequence is intuitive: metahistory dissolves into empirical history. In so far as human nature is symbolized by social and political praxis, it becomes a petulant and superfluous myth. Isn't this the position of hermeneutics and, at least in part, of Foucault? To a history-as-index and a history-as-symbol, we need to oppose with equal decision *history-as-icon*.

b) Natural history is the materialist, rigorously atheistic version of theological Revelation. Just as Christian faith is founded on the empirical fact of the incarnation of an eternal God in a mortal body, natural history rests on the empirical fact of the manifestation of the biological invariant social and political praxis. In both cases, metahistory acquires a contingent aspect without ceasing to exist. Be it a Creator or simply the phylogenetic prerogatives of the human animal, something inalterable appears in a fragile *hic and nunc*, coming to the fore as phenomenon among phenomena, assuming an aspect that could also have been other. The Son could have had different hands, or a different physiognomy, just as the historical manifestation of neoteny can assume a completely different form. The revelation of human nature, just as the Christian *parousia*, is fully traversed by particular circumstances and political conflicts: it does not occur despite the circumstances, but thanks to them. The state of affairs in which the implicit becomes explicit is unique and irreproducible, that is, quintessentially historical. It is obvious that for natural history, what is revealed is not God, but the unchanging biological nature of our species, be it the innate linguistic faculty or the genetic lack of a specific environment. Furthermore, this revelation brings no salvation: its concrete mediation, such as the flexibility of contemporary production, is far from messianic.

Natural historiography, after having metabolized and reinterpreted the logic of revelation, fundamentally dethrones transcendental philosophy. These two thoughts are mutually exclusive precisely because they are co-extensive, that is, because they treat the same problem in antithetical ways. The relation between eternity and contingency, invariant and change, presuppositions of experience and empirical phenomena can be seriously conceived only according to a transcendental or a historic-naturalistic interpretation. The legitimacy of one approach implies the ruin of the other. This contrast does not verge on the existence of transcendental categories. Naturalist historiography recognizes without hesitation that the linguistic faculty is the a priori condition of all discourse, and also, less obviously, that this immutable condition possesses specific characteristics that are very different from changing conditions. The contrast, in fact, is centered on the possible empirical manifestation of transcendence, that is, the possible revelation of eternity in contingency. Natural historiography, which finds its strength in this revelatory manifestation, affirms that the presuppositions of experience can constitute the object of *direct experience.*

Transcendental philosophy prides itself in affirming that the presuppositions of human praxis, which determine facts and states of affairs, never appear as facts or states of affairs themselves. Presuppositions remain hidden in their prefix, without ever being "posited." What founds or allows all appearance does not appear. The visual field cannot be seen, historicity does not fall in the realm of historical events, the linguistic faculty cannot be enunciated ("that which expresses itself in language, we cannot express by language.").[37] Naturalist historiography, which adopts a logic of revelation, rebukes these positions, without neglecting or despising the preoccupations that found them. This means that we are far from reducing the variant to the invariant, from equating the visual field to the sum of visible things, or from mistaking historicity for a collection of historical facts. Rather, naturalist historiography shows that transcendence, *while maintaining its prerogatives*, does dispose of a specific phenomenal correspondent. There are empirical phenomena that exactly reproduce the structure of transcendence, tracing either its image or its diagram. Besides being its presupposition, the invariant appears as such in certain variable states of affairs. Not only does it allow for the most variable events, but it too occurs in time, assuming an evental physiognomy. The invariant presupposition acquires its own facticity, becoming a *post*-posited. There are historical conjunctures (cultural apocalypses and so forth) that show, between the lines, the presuppositions of history itself. There are aspects of our most banal enunciations that emphasize the indeterminate linguistic faculty; there are formulas that adequately express "that which expresses itself in language." In a certain sense, therefore, there are visible objects that show in themselves their own visual field. Transcendental foundations, which make all appearances possible, appear themselves: in fact, it lets itself be seen, attracts the gaze, stages its own manifestation becoming even more than apparent in its startling images.

Let us think again of the dispute between Foucault and Chomsky on human nature, and of the two antagonistic choices that came into conflict: the dissolution of metahistory in empirical history (Foucault), or the reabsorption of history in invariable metahistory (Chomsky). Naturalist historiography, radically unhappy with both positions, presents the alternative of *historicizing metahistory*. Of course, thinking that metahistory assumes historical semblances and expresses itself factually and contingently, is equivalent to assuming that transcendence is visible, disposing of an empirical correspondent. Just as the manifestation of transcendence does not imply its abrogation, the historicization of metahistory is far from postulating its annihilation or even its relativist weakening. I repeat once again what by now should be clear: historicizing metahistory simply means reconstructing how, while remaining effectively invariant, it surfaces in historical events, constituting an operative field for social praxis. This is far more complicated and interesting than trying to exorcize the notion of "human nature." On the other hand, precisely because it appears in the factual-empirical field, becoming the object of political conflicts, metahistory cannot reabsorb the variations of contingent history, nor can it dictate the ideal of a just society.

We saw that the two theoretical options of Eindhoven are objectively related to a mythical-religious horizon. The attempt to dissolve metahistory (human nature, innate speaking ability, neoteny and so on) in social and political history is punished by reappearance or the strengthening of religious passions. The invariable "always already," separated from historical materialism, is left to theology. On the other hand, the pretense of reabsorbing the mercurial "just now" in metahistory ends up by retracing the mythical instance of a return to the origins. The immutable archetype, that should determine the unmanageable proliferation of historical events, fulfills a clear apotropaic task. Natural history, historicizing metahistory, escapes the mythical-religious horizon and does not expose itself to a religious punishment giving its just importance to biological metahistory. It doesn't unwittingly repeat the mythical model of a reduction of becoming to archetypes, since it preserves the contingency of historical events (actually emphasizing the historical-contingent aspect that sometimes befalls to phylogenetic metahistory itself). Naturalist historiography, therefore, is *atheistic.* In this context, atheism is defined logically, not as a psychological whim or a polemic reaction. Far from remaining a nineteenth-century lamentation, atheism coincides with the affirmed empirical appearance of transcendence: it coincides with an exponential empiricism able to reclaim even the presuppositions of experience. But then, one could possibly object, why did we want to establish a relation between natural history and a theology of revelation? The reason is quite simple: the idea of revelation implies the radical overcoming of theology, while remaining in the theological field. This is not any kind of overcoming, but the only credible and logical one.

Only if they assume an empirical and contingent form, and are not hurriedly pushed aside, can metahistory and transcendence abandon all religious appearance. The phenomenal revelation of the biological invariant makes impossible both its reduction to an archetype determining all new becoming, and its elevation to a cultic object as inscrutable "supplement" of power and productive relations. In other words, it neutralizes two truly religious options. This is why the theology of revelation is of some interest for the integral empiricism (logically atheistic) of natural history. This is not irrelevant.

c) When we speak of esthetical or chemical phenomena, we make an implicit recourse to a selective criterion in order to qualify and circumscribe the object in question. The same is true for historical-natural phenomena. They don't coincide with the totality of historical or natural phenomena, but they configure a precise field where they fully interact. This is the field where history, in its most historical aspect (verbal language, labor, politics), reflects without any mediation the most irreducibly natural, that is culturally unchangeable, aspects of human nature. What denotes historical-natural phenomena and sets them aside from all others is a quite specific array of requirements. After having examined them one by one, we can now give their complete list, so that their mutual relations and implications may become clear.

Historical-natural phenomena are *iconic*. We are dealing with contingent events that nonetheless provide us with the image or the diagram of an immutable, species-specific structure. They are never its indexes (that is, its consequence) nor its symbol.

Historical-natural phenomena are *revelatory*. They attribute an undeniable social and ethical preeminence to the biological invariant. They bring the background to the fore, they make extrinsic what was intrinsic and the implicit explicit. They give political relevance to what seemed an obscure metahistorical premise: the linguistic faculty (potential and biological), the non-specialization of the human animal, neoteny and the difference between "world" and "environment."

Historical-natural phenomena are *transcendental*. What at first blush can seem a contradiction is in fact the expression of a decisive philosophical issue: the visibility (or facticity) of transcendence. Historical-natural phenomena imply the possibility of experiencing the presuppositions of experience.

Historical-natural phenomena are *reflexive*. They coincide with the occasions for historical praxis to stage as content, or operative field, those biological presuppositions (potentiality, neoteny and so on) that allow the existence of something like a "historical praxis." In historical-natural phenomena, the species looks back on itself or, in other words, retraces the crucial stages of anthropogenesis. This is what Marx alludes to when he writes that we arrive at a moment when human nature becomes the object of sensorial perception. In order to avoid misunderstandings, however, we need to include a note of caution: what makes historical-natural phenomena reflexive is not our consciousness. The transcendental prejudice needs to be abandoned also in this respect. In fact, it is the intrinsic reflexivity of these phenomena that encourages and facilitates certain reflexive, conscious operations.

Finally, historical-natural phenomena are *transindividual*. They make visible the incomplete nature of the individual mind. This incompleteness can never be saturated by the single individual, and therefore sends us back, from the beginning, to collective praxis, that is, to what happens "among" individuals (without belonging to anyone in particular). The individual mind, in its original biological constitution, is always more than individual: it is transindividual and, even better, public. Historical-natural phenomena illustrate the innate public nature of the human mind. To the extrinsic character of the I Marx alludes when he writes the industry is the making present of human psychology or when, in a later text, he talks about a "social individual."

d) Natural history as such doesn't found or support any politics. Any attempt to deduce from it certain goals and tactics would be abusive and naïve. Still, it is true that natural history indicates with precision what the terrain of political conflict really is. In other words, it formulates the most important questions for which there might be radical alternatives and violent conflicts. All political theories have to contend with cultural apocalypses and the empirical revelation of metahistory. But they do so in the name of contrasting interests. All political theories pay the highest attention to the situations when human praxis focuses most directly on what renders such praxis "human." But this common attention produces antipodal responses, whose realization depends on power relations, and not on their degree of adherence to "human nature." Politics in general, and today more than ever, finds its raw material in historical-natural phenomena, that is, in the contingent events that reveal the distinctive traits of our species. The raw materials, though, and not a paradigm or an inspiring principle.

It is useless to appeal, like Chomsky does, to the inalterable biological patrimony of *Homo sapiens* in order to rectify the injustices of contemporary capitalism. Today, rather than being the springboard and the inspiration for a possible emancipation, our innate linguistic creativity manifests itself as a component of the despotic organization of work. In fact, it appears as a profitable economic resource. In so far as it achieves an immediate empirical consistency, the biological invariant is part of the problem, not the solution. Both the politics perpetuating the oppression, and those that want to end it, are familiar with the incarnations of metahistory in contingent facts. The difference between the two, then, resides in the *various* forms that the "always already" can acquire in the "just now." It is an irreversible fact that the innate potential of the human animal appears in the economic-social field is an irreversible fact, but that this potential should assume the aspect of marketable labor is not an inescapable destiny. In fact, it is only a transient occurrence that is worth opposing *politically*. We need to assume that the transindividuality of the human mind necessarily becomes a factual evidence, but this does not mean that it has to conform to the necessities of post-fordist industry. In the same way, we don't need to believe that the icon of the biological non-specialization of the human animal will continue to be the servile flexibility that is the pride and joy of contemporary labor processes. This is also true, of course, of all the other properties of historical-natural phenomena. Naturalist historiography does not diminish the importance and the fragile dignity of political action: it increases it exponentially.

7

The Multitude and the Principle of Individuation[1]

1. The One and the many

Contemporary forms of life bear witness to the dissolution of the concept of "people" and the renewed pertinence of the concept of "multitude." These two concepts, which where the guiding stars of the great sixteenth-century debate that gave rise to a good part of our ethical-political vocabulary, are completely antithetic. The "people" has a centripetal nature, it converges in a volonté générale, is the interface or the emanation of the State; the "multitude" is plural, eschews political unity, doesn't stipulate contracts or transfer its rights to the sovereign, it resists obedience and is inclined towards non-representative democratic forms. Hobbes saw in the multitude the greatest danger for the State apparatus ("stirring up the citizens against the city, that is to say, the multitude against the people"),[2] Spinoza the origins of freedom. From the sixteenth century onwards, almost without exception, "the people" has unconditionally prevailed. The political existence of the many as many has been expunged from the horizon of modernity not only by the theoreticians of the absolute State, but also by Rousseau, traditional liberalism and the socialist movement itself. Today, however, the multitude takes its revenge, characterizing all aspects of social life:

habits and theories of post-fordist labor, language games, passions and affects, ways of understanding collective action. When we analyze this revenge, we need to avoid at least a couple of idiocies. It is not the case that the working class happily went extinct to make room for the "many": rather—and this is a much more complicated and interesting problem—it has remained the same but no longer has the aspect of a people, while perfectly exemplifying the way of being of the multitude. Secondly, saying that the "many" characterize contemporary forms of life has nothing idyllic about it: they characterize them both positively and negatively, promoting servility as well as conflict. We are dealing with a form of life, certainly different from the "popular" but nonetheless rather ambivalent, since it possesses *its own* poisons.

The multitude doesn't nonchalantly get rid of the issue concerning the universals, the common/shared, the One, but requalifies it completely. First of all, we assist to a reversal in the order of the components: the people tends towards the One, while the many derive from it. For the people, universality is a *promise*, for the many it is a *premise*. The people gravitate towards the One of the State, of the Sovereign, of the *volonté générale*. The multitude is backed up by the One of language, by the intellect as public or inter-psychological resource, and the generic faculties of the species. If the multitude refuses the unity of the State it is only because it relates to a completely different One. This relation, that I have already discussed elsewhere,[3] has to be explored further.

As we have already said, an important contribution is offered by Gilbert Simondon, a philosopher dear to Deleuze who has remained almost unknown in Italy. His reflection focuses on the principles of individuation. The passage from the generic psychosomatic patrimony of the human animal to the configuration of a unique singularity is the most important category for the multitude. If we think about it, the category of the people is more pertinent to a myriad non-individuated individuals taken as simple substances or solipsistic atoms. Precisely because they constitute an immediate starting point, and not the extreme result of a difficult trajectory, these individuals need the unity/universality provided by the State apparatus. On the contrary, when we speak about the multitude, we focus on the process of individuation, that is, on the derivation of each "many" from a certain unity/universality. Simondon, like the Russian psychologist Vygotsky and the Italian anthropologist Ernesto De Martino, focused precisely on this type of derivation. For these thinkers, ontogenesis, or the development of the single self-conscious "I" is a *philosophia prima*, the only perspicuous analysis of being and becoming, because it coincides fully with the "principle of individuation." Individuation allows us to conceive the other relation One/many that we were discussing earlier, which does not see the One as coinciding with the State. Ontogenesis is a category that contributes to the foundation of the ethico-political notion of multitude.

Gaston Bachelard, one of the greatest epistemologists of the twentieth century, wrote that quantic physics is a "grammatical subject" which needs to be described with the most heterogeneous philosophical "predicates": if a single problem can be defined in Humean terms, another might need a sentence taken from Hegelian logic or a notion taken from Gestalt psychology. Similarly, the way of being of the multitude has to be qualified with attributes coming from very different, even contradictory contexts. They can be found, for instance, in Gehlen's philosophical anthropology (biological insufficiency of the human being, lack of a well-defined "environment," scarce specialized instincts), in the pages of *Being and Time* devoted to everyday life (chatter, curiosity, misunderstandings and so on), or in Wittgenstein's description of language games in his *Philosophical Investigations.* These are all objectionable examples, but the importance of Simondon's two theses as predicates of the concept of multitude is incontrovertible: a) the subject is always an incomplete and partial individuation, consisting in a changing network of pre-individual and actually singular traits; b) collective experience, far from signaling the decadence and the eclipse of individuation, refines and continues it. We can't treat all relevant aspects (including the fundamental question of *how*, according to Simondon, individuation is realized), but it is worth focusing on these rather counter-intuitive and even controversial theses.

2. Pre-individual

Let us start from the beginning. The multitude is a network of individuals. The term "many" indicates a group of contingent singularities. These singularities, however, are not an uncontroversial fact, but the complex result of a process of individuation. It is obvious that the starting for any true individuation is something that is *not* quite individual *yet.* What is unique, unrepeatable, fragile, comes from what is undifferentiated and generic. The specific characters of individuality are rooted in a series of universal paradigms. Just by talking about the *principium individuationis* we postulate a rock-solid relation between the singular and some form of anonymous force. The individual is such not because it remains in the margins of power, like a revengeful and bloodless zombie, but because it is individuated power only as one of the possible individuations of power.

When he defines the premises of individuation, Simondon uses the very clear notion of preindividual reality. All the many are familiar with this antithetic polarity. But what is the preindividual? Simondon writes:

> We could call nature this pre-individual reality that the individual brings with itself, trying to find in the word "nature" the meaning attributed to it by pre-socratic philosophers: the Ionic physiologists saw in it all the different kinds of being preceding individuation; nature is the reality of the possible, presenting the traits of that *apeiron* which, according to Anaximander, is the origin of all individuated forms. Nature is not the opposite of Man, but the first stage of being, while the second is the opposition between individual and environment.[4]

Nature, *apeiron* (undetermined), reality of the possible, a being still without stages: we could continue. But we can already propose an autonomous definition of "pre-individual," which does not contradict Simondon's but is independent from it. It is not hard to recognize that under the same label different fields and levels can coexist.

First of all, we call pre-individual sensorial perception, motility, and the biological foundation of the species. Merleau-Ponty, in his *Phenomenology of Perception*, observed that "I am no more aware of being the true subject of my sensations more than I am of my birth and my death."[5] He continues saying that "sight, hearing, touch, with their fields [...] are anterior, and remain alien, to my personal life."[6] Sensation eschews first-person descriptions: when I perceive, it is not the individuated individual who perceives, but the species as such. Only the anonymous pronoun "one" can describe motility and sensibility: *one* sees, *one* hears, *one* feels pain or pleasure. It is true that perception sometimes acquires a *self-reflexive* aspect: touching, for instance, is always a being touched by the object we are handling. The one who perceives feels him or herself while he or she is reaching toward the object. But this self-reference lacks individuation. The species feels itself in the act of handling, not a self-conscious singularity. It is a mistake to identify two different concepts, affirming that where there is self-reflection there is also a process of individuation, or, vice versa, that if there is no individuation we cannot speak of self-reflexivity.

At a more precise level, we call pre-individual the historico-natural language of one's community. A particular language inheres to all the speakers in a given community, just like an animal "environment" or an enveloping and undifferentiated amniotic fluid. Linguistic communication is intersubjective long before the formation of true "subjects." Belonging to everybody and nobody at the same time, it is also best described by the anonymous "one." Vygotsky underscored more than anyone else the pre-individual, immediately social nature of human speech: the use of language, at the beginning, is inter-psychic, that is, public, shared, impersonal. Contrary to what Piaget thought, we don't need to overcome an originally autistic (or hyper-individual) condition entering the path of socialization; on the contrary, the focus of ontogenesis, according to Vygotsky, consists in passing from a total sociality to the individuation of the speaker. Vygotsky's recognition of the pre-individual aspects of language anticipates Wittgenstein's confutation of all "private languages"; furthermore, and this is what counts most, Vygotsky can be included in the small list of thinkers who have focused on the *principium individuationis*. For him, just as for Simondon, psychological individuation (that is, the constitution of the self-conscious I) happens in the linguistic field, not in perception. In other words: while the pre-individual of the sensation seems destined to remain such forever, the pre-individual aspect of language can instead differentiate itself internally giving rise to individuality. We have already talked about the ways in which, according to Simondon and Vygotsky, the singularization of the speaker takes place, and we also explained how their hypotheses could be supplemented. What is important is to underscore the separation between the perceptive field, which is a biological attribute without individuation, and the linguistic one, which is the basis of individuation.

And finally, *pre-individual* is the production process of a certain era. In advanced capitalism, the labor process mobilizes the most universal aspects of the species: perception, language, memory, affects. Roles and tasks, in the postfordist era, coincide largely with the "generic existence," the *Gattungswesen* described by Marx and Feuerbach in *The Economic and Philosophic Manuscripts of 1844* with regard to the most basic faculties of the human species. Productive processes are all pre-individual, but thought is particularly important. We are talking, of course, of the kind of objective thought, unrelated to a certain psychological "I," whose truth does not depend from the assent of single individuals. This is what Gottlob Frege called "thought without a subject," in a rather raw but effective formula. Marx created the famous and controversial definition of general intellect, but for him, the general intellect (abstract knowledge, science, impersonal knowledge) is also the pillar of wealth creation. Wealth, in this sense, has to be understood as absolute and relative plus value. Subject-less thought, that is, the general intellect, imposes its form on society's vital processes, instituting hierarchies and power relations. In other words: it is a historically qualified pre-individual reality. We don't need to insist on this point, but let's remember that to the perceptual and a linguistic pre-individuality, we need to add the historical one.

3. An amphibious subject

The subject does not coincide with the individuated individual, but always includes a certain ratio of pre-individual reality. It is an unstable, impure composite. Here is the first thesis by Simondon that I want to emphasize: "there is in individuated beings a certain measure of indeterminacy, that is, of pre-individual reality that went through the process of individuation without actually being individuated. This measure of indeterminacy can be called nature."[7] It is wrong to reduce the subject to what is singular: "We mistakenly call an individual a more complex reality, the one of the whole subject, who in addition to his or her individual reality also maintains a non-individuated, pre-individual, that is, natural aspect."[8] The pre-individual is mostly felt as a non-resolved past, the reality of the possible that gave birth to the well-defined singularity and still remains at its side: diachrony does not exclude concomitance. On another note, the pre-individual traversing the subject manifests itself as the environment of the individuated individual. The environmental context (perception, language, history) of the singular experience is indeed an intrinsic (or inner) component of the subject. The subject does not *have* an environment, but, at least in its non-individuated part, *is* it. From Locke to Fodor, the philosophies that ignore the pre-individual reality of the subject, neglecting what *in* it is its environment, are destined to find no relation between "internal" and "external," between the I and world. They fall into the trap denounced by Simondon: they equate the subject with the individuated individual.

The notion of subjectivity is amphibious: the "I speak" coexists with the "one speaks": the un-repeatable is tied to what is serial and recurrent. Or, more precisely: in the texture of the subject there appear, as integral components, the anonymous voice of perception (sensation as species-specific sensation), the inter-psychic or "public" aspect of the native tongue, and the participation of the impersonal general intellect. According to Simondon, the coexistence of the pre-individual and the individuated within the subject is mediated by our affects. Passions and emotions express the temporary integration of these two aspects. But they can also get separated: there can be crises, recessions, catastrophes. We experience panic, or anxiety, when we cannot bring together the pre-individual and the individuated aspects of our experience:

> When anxious, the subject feels its own existence as a problem, he feels his double nature of pre-individual and individuated being; the individuated being is *here and now*, and *this here and this now* prevent the manifestation of an infinite number of other *here* and *now*: the subject becomes conscious of itself as nature, as the indeterminate (*apeiron*) incapable of realizing itself in a *hic and nunc*, incapable of living.[9]

We can observe an extraordinary coincidence between Simondon's analysis and De Martino's diagnosis of cultural apocalypse. The main point, for both of them, is that ontogenesis, that is individuation, is never guaranteed: it can regress, become weaker and even explode. The "I think," besides having a rather difficult genesis, is partially reversible, overwhelmed by what happens to it. According to De Martino, sometimes pre-individuality overwhelms the singular I: the latter is sucked into the anonymity of the "one." At other times, in a symmetrically opposite manner, we try in vain to reduce all the pre-individual aspects of our existence to the specific singularity. These two pathologies are only the most extreme manifestations of an oscillation that, in more moderate forms, is constant and inevitable.

Too often, the critical thought of the twentieth century (for instance, the Frankfurt School) has complained about the presumed distance between the individual and the productive forces, as well as its separation from the potential of the universal faculties of the species (language, thought and so on). The causes of unhappiness were precisely this distance and separation. This is a fascinating but wrong idea. "Sad passions," as Spinoza called them, arise in fact from the extreme proximity, actually from the symbiosis between the individuated individual and the pre-individual when there is an imbalance, a laceration between the two. For good or bad, the multitude is composed of an inextricable texture of "I" and "one," of unique singularity and the anonymity of the species. The good part is that each of the "many," being backed by the universal as premise and precedent, doesn't need the artificial universality of the State. The bad part is that each of the "many," as amphibious subject, can always see its own pre-individual reality as a threat, or at least a source of insecurity. The ethico-political concept of multitude is rooted *both* in the principle of individuation *and* in its constitutive incompleteness.

4. Marx, Vygotsky, Simondon: the concept of "social individual"

In a famous passage of the *Grundrisse* that we have already quoted, Marx says that the "social individual" is the only credible protagonist of all radical change of the present state of affairs. At first sight, the definition "social individual" seems a superficial oxymoron, a confusing union of opposites, or even a Hegelian mannerism. Instead, we should take this concept literally, and use it as a tool precisely calibrated to retrace contemporary ways of being, trends and life forms. But this is only possible, to a great extent, thanks to Simondon's and Vygotsky's reflection on the principle of individuation.

In the adjective "social" we need to recognize the features of that pre-individual reality that according to Simondon is inherent to all subjects, just as the name "individual" designates the singularization of each member of today's multitude. When speaking of the social individual, Marx is referring to the relation between "generic existence" (*Gattungswesen*) and the unrepeatable experience constituting the seal of subjectivity. It is not by chance that the social individual appears in the same part of the *Grundrisse* where we find the notion of a general intellect constituting the universal (or pre-individual) premise and the common score for the labor and life of the "many." The social aspect of the "social individual" is undoubtedly the general intellect, that Frege called thought without a subject. It is also, however, the immediately inter-psychic, public aspect of human communication, that was recognized with great intelligence by Vygotsky. Furthermore, if we rightly conflate the "social" with the "pre-individual," we will have to acknowledge that the individuated individual discussed by Marx is also configured against the background of our anonymous sensorial perceptions.

Social, in the stronger sense, is both the historically defined productive forces and the biological attributes of the species. This is not an external relation or a simple overlap. There is more: fully realized capitalism implies a total coincidence between productive forces and the other two types of pre-individual realities (the "one perceives" and the "one speaks"). The concept of labor potential shows this perfect fusion: as generic physical and linguistic-intellectual ability to produce, the potential to work is to a certain degree historically determined, but it also includes all the *apeiron*, the non-individuated nature, described by Simondon, as well as the impersonal aspect of language exhaustively illustrated by Vygotsky. The "social individual" marks an era when the coexistence of the singular and the pre-individual is no longer a heuristic hypothesis or a hidden presupposition, but has become an empirical phenomenon, a truth that has come to the surface, a pragmatic given. We could say that anthropogenesis, that is, the very constitution of the human animal, has started to appear on the socio-historical plane, has become visible, and has been subjected to a kind of materialistic revelation. The so-called "transcendental conditions of experience," rather than remaining in the background, have come to the fore and, even more importantly, have also become the object of immediate experience.

A last remark: the social individual incorporates the universal productive forces but only articulates them in specific and contingent ways. In fact, it becomes individuated precisely by configuring them in a singular manner, translating them in a very specific constellation of affects and knowledge. This is why all attempts at negatively defining the individual are destined to fail: it can only be described by the intensity of what it absorbs, nor by all that is excluded from it. This is not an accidental and unregulated, ineffable positivity (and by the way, nothing is more monotonous and less individual than the ineffable). Individuation is characterized by a progressive specification and by the ex-centric combination of general rules and paradigms. It is not a whole in the net, but the place where its texture is the tightest. When talking about the unrepeatable singularity, we could speak of a *surplus of legislation*. In epistemic terms, the laws qualifying the universal are neither "universal assertions" (valid for all the occurrences of a homogeneous array of phenomena) nor "existential affirmations" (the simple collection of empirical data outside of all regularity or connective scheme): these are truly *singular laws.* They are laws because they possess a formal structure virtually consisting of a whole species. They are singular because they apply to a single case. Singular laws represent the individual with the precision and the transparency normally reserved to a logical "class": but this class consists of only one individual.

I call "multitude" the totality of "social individuals." There is a valuable semantic concatenation between the political existence of the many as many, the old philosophic question concerning the *principium individuationis*, and the Marxian notion of social individual (interpreted, with the help of Simondon, as the inextricable relation between contingent singularity and pre-individual reality). This semantic concatenation allows us to radically redefine the nature and the functions of the public sphere and of collective action. This redefinition, of course, destroys the ethico-political canon founded on the "people" and State sovereignty. We could say—with Marx but outside and against a good part of Marxist ideology—that the substance of our hopes consist in attributing the utmost importance and value to the unrepeatable existence of every member of the species. As paradoxical as it may seem, today Marx should be read as a rigorous, that is, realistic and complex, theorist of the individual and, therefore, of *individuation.*

5. Multitude and collectivity

Let us analyze, now, Simondon's second thesis, which is completely unprecedented and is counter-intuitive, that is, it goes against many deeply seated, common sense convictions (as it is the case, in fact, for many of the predicates pertaining to the multitude). Usually we think that as soon as an individual enters a collectivity it has to abandon at least some of its individual characteristics, giving up certain colorful and mysterious distinctive signs. Apparently, a singularity fades away in a collectivity, it is mutilated and diminished. But according to Simondon, this is an epistemologically flawed and ethically suspicious prejudice. This prejudice is fomented by those who, happily forgetting the issue of individuation, assume that the individual is an immediate starting point. But if we admit that the individual originates in its opposite, that is, the undifferentiated universal, the problem of collectivity assumes a completely different aspect. According to Simondon, contrary to what our deformed common sense might tell us, collective life is the opportunity for a further, more complex individuation. Far from regressing, the singularity reaches its highest level in common action, in the plurality of voices and, finally, in the common sphere.

Collectivity does not prevent or diminish individuation, but it continues it in a more powerful way. This continuation concerns the ratio of pre-individual reality that the first process of individuation had left unresolved. Simondon writes:

> We should not talk about an individual preference for group life, because these preferences are not, properly speaking, individual; they are the non-resolution of the potentials preceding the genesis of the individual. The being preceding the individual has not been individuate without leaving a residue; it has not been completely resolved in an individual and in an environment; the individual has kept something pre-individual, so that all the individuals share a kind of unstructured background that can lead to a new individuation.[10]

And he also adds that "it is not really as individuals that in a collectivity beings relate to one another, but as subjects, that is as beings that possess something pre-individual."[11] The group rests on the pre-individual element (one perceives, one speaks and so on) present in every subject. But in a group the pre-individual reality, enmeshed with different singularities, also becomes individuated, assuming a specific physiognomy.

The instance of the collectivity is also a kind of individuation: the stakes are the imposition of a contingent and recognizable form to the *apeiron* (the undetermined), that is, to the reality of the possible preceding the singularity; to the anonymous universe of sensorial perception; to the thought without thinker or the general intellect. The pre-individual, surviving within the isolated subject, can singularize itself in the actions and emotions of the many, just as the cellist playing in a quartet with other musicians, grasps an aspect of the score that previously had eluded him. Each of the "many" personalizes (partially and temporarily) its own impersonal component through the typical vicissitudes of public life. Being exposed to the gaze of the other, the risks of political action, the familiarity with the possible and the unforeseen, friendships and enmities: all of this affords to the individual the opportunity to take some ownership of the "one" whence it originates, transforming the *Gattungswesen*, the generic existence of the species, in a unique biography. Contrary to what Heidegger thought, only in the public sphere can we go from the "one" to "oneself."

Second-degree individuation, that Simondon also calls "collective individuation" (an oxymoron similar to the one contained in the expression "social individual"), is an important step in adequately thinking non-representative democracy. Since the collectivity is the stage for an emphasized singularization of experience, constituting the place where what is incommensurable and unique in every human life can express itself, nothing in it can be extrapolated or, even worse, "delegated." But let's be careful: the collectivity of the multitude, as individuation of the general intellect and the biological basis of the species, is the opposite of any form of naïve anarchism. When compared to it, it is the model of political representation, with its concepts of volonté general and "popular sovereignty," that look like an intolerable (and sometimes ferocious) simplification. The collectivity of the multitude doesn't enter into any covenant, nor does it transfer its right to a sovereign, because it is composed of individuated singularities: the universal is not a promise, but a premise.

Appendix

Wittgenstein and the Question of Atheism

1. Blasphemous metaphysics

Recalling from time to time Wittgenstein's critique of metaphysics, and even of philosophy tout court, is an innocuous, inevitable and recurring physiognomic tic. It also resembles a polite formula, something like "How are you?," a question that does not expect an answer and aims simply at establishing a connection with the interlocutor. Both the tic and the formula are perspicuous, of course: Wittgenstein never stopped asking the same question. At the same time, we are left to wonder whether the systematic dissolution of the traditional questions of metaphysics, operated in the name of the effective functioning of our language, derives from an *empiricist-naturalist* or a *religious* perspective. In the following remarks, we would like to support the second hypothesis. When examined closely, one sees how Wittgenstein's fury against "false problems" is a protest against the irreverence, or rather, the inevitably blasphemous character of metaphysics. The elimination of philosophical puzzles is similar to the rigorous respect of the ancient admonition: "don't invoke the name of God in vain."

Contrary to what one might suppose, religion doesn't contradict the empiricist-naturalist perspective, but actually supports and intensifies it. Since God cannot be named in vain, and nothing meaningful can be said about "the meaning of life," it is finally possible to get rid of any house of cards coming between the earthly tasks of our language and the ineffable ("what really counts"). We can then focus on verbal language as simple biological faculty of *Homo sapiens*. The religious critique of metaphysics coincides largely with the most radical and intransigent naturalism. And in fact, something of the sort had happened in Schelling's case, in the solid alliance that he established between anti-metaphysical empiricism and theological revelation.

Wittgenstein's incessant struggle against blasphemy: this is the theme of the following remarks. These are just very quick notes, of course. These are notes made for oneself and one's readers, waiting for a future development. First of all, a word of warning: the religious critique of metaphysics has little to do with the author's biography or with the convoluted spirals of his psychological life. Neither is it an esoteric indication coming from a "secret journal." Rather, it sits in plain view, like Poe's purloined letter, and calls into question fundamental notions, such as "limit" and "self-reference." We need to ask ourselves: what is the logical form of Wittgenstein's texts? Both in the *Tractatus* and in the *Philosophical Investigations* the argument gravitates around the relation between sayable and unsayable, that is, between sense and nonsense. But we assist to a progressive radicalization: in the *Tractatus* there prevails the Kantian sublime: the unrepresentable is shown through the clash between representation and its blind spot. In the *Investigations*, instead, we see the development of a coherent asceticism, where the drastic separation between the "penultimate" (the ordinary usage of language) and the "ultimate" (the meaning of life, that is, what really counts) reigns supreme.

The argumentative structure of the *Tractatus* is explained very clearly in the 1930 *Lecture on Ethics* that Wittgenstein gave in Cambridge to the members of the "Heretics" circle. This text, linear in appearance only, can be considered a sort of retrospective *discours de la méthode*. It is far more difficult, however, to find an *organon* for the work that Wittgenstein did after 1930. There is an intrinsic reason for this difficulty: it is precisely the higher level of asceticism that implies the absence—and this time absolute—of any meta-discourse, that is, of any "ladder" to be thrown away after its usage. Still, we can find a few indications in the paragraphs 93–133 of the *Investigations*.

If the form of the *Tractatus* (in other words, the "proclamation of silence") can be illustrated through the "Analytic of the sublime" in Kant's *Critique of Judgment*, the logical form of the *Investigations* (that we could call "the practice of silence") finds an adequate correspondence in the most radical negative theology of our time, such as the one practiced by Simone Weil or by the Lutheran Dietrich Bonhoeffer, hung by the Nazis in 1945. Tellingly, the first work is still tied to a fundamental text of our philosophical tradition, while in order to understand the second one (which is completely antimetaphysical and constitutes the guiding star of contemporary analytic philosophy) we need an explicit reference to mystical experience.

2. The sublime as logical form of the *Tractatus*

The feeling of the sublime, according to Kant, originates in our inclination to see in natural phenomena the image of what lies beyond nature. Or more precisely, it comes from the attempt to derive from some earthly event a figure of the world as a complete whole. The pretense of showing empirically the transcendent ideas of reasons (and first of all the idea of the world) is irrevocably destined to fail. However, this pretense allows us to represent the catastrophe of representation. It is the staging of this catastrophe that gestures—although negatively—towards a higher truth. The experienced inadequacy of any image constitutes the only possible "image" of the extra-sensorial: it indexes it as what lies outside the visual field.

In his *Lecture on Ethics*, Wittgenstein compares the ethical feeling to a "miracle." It coincides perfectly with the Kantian sublime.[1] First of all, is miraculous the wonder we experience faced with the existence of the world ("Not how the world is, is the mystical, but that it is").[2] This surprise is the result of an effort and, at the same time, of its failure. It is the effort to look at the world from the outside (as the complete totality discussed by Kant), and the failure due to the impossibility to go beyond the realm to which we are bound. Without the effort, or in the case of its success, there would be no wonder. The latter becomes an educational frustration. Just as it happened for the sublime, in the experience of the miracle the ruin of exposition corresponds with what we wanted to expose. We can address God only with senseless words that fully show how "God does not reveal himself in the world."[3]

For Wittgenstein, the wonder caused by the existence of the world is indistinguishable from the one caused by the existence of language. A meaningful discourse cannot account for the world's existence for the same reasons that prevent it from accounting for its own presence: "now I am tempted to say that the right expression in language for the miracle of the existence of the world, though it is not any proposition *in* language, is the existence of language itself."[4] If we could express in words the linguistic faculty itself, then we could dispose of the terms able to describe the world as totality. But according to Wittgenstein, this is impossible: language can never account for itself, since "that which expresses itself in language, we cannot express by language."[5] This is why, "by shifting the expression of the miraculous from an expression by means of language to the expression by the existence of language, all I have said is again that we cannot express what we want to express and that all we say about the absolute miraculous remains nonsense."[6]

The cosmological question (considering the world as a limited totality) shares fully the structure and the aporias of linguistic self-reference (where what is at stake is not what we say, but the fact of speech itself). When we try to say something meaningful about the existence of the world, we are also trying to look at the dark side of language, representing it from the outside. Both attempts are destined to fail. Both language and the world refer to each other, like the first two figures of the Christian trinity: during a conversation with Friederich Waismann, when the latter had asked whether the existence of the world was related to ethics, Wittgenstein answered that the relation was attested by the fact that "men had felt it and expressed it such: 'the Father created the world, the Son (or the Word, that from which God emanates) is the Ethical."[7]

The sublime, that is, the logical form of the *Tractatus*, is founded on the concept of limit. This limit is twofold: "the limits of my language mean the limits of my world."[8] A the end of the Lecture on Ethics, Wittgenstein recognizes that when he was talking about the absolute good and the meaning of life, he was proposing "to go beyond the world and *that is to say* beyond significant language."[9] Metaphysics thinks that it can venture beyond the world with the help of language. A religious critique of metaphysics, on the other hand, is rooted in the identity of the limit imposed upon both concepts. If world and language are co-extensive, their "beyond" is the same: neither worldly nor linguistic, it inevitably assumes a theological aspect. Self-reference is the opportunity—quintessentially sublime—to represent the catastrophe of representation trying to go beyond its limits, and to think God negatively as what would be blasphemous to name.

Equating world and language, limits common to the two terms, self-reference as educational frustration: these are the three key notions—logical, and not biographical-psychological—that found, at the time of the *Tractatus*, the religious liquidation of the irreverent babbling of philosophy. From these notions we can infer that the world (*Welt*) of the human animal is not an environment (*Umwelt*), and also that having a world implies an absolutely ineffable reference to a *Deus absconditus* (the indivisible unity of the Father-Creator and the Son-Word). Let us analyze this double inference in more depth.

A zoological "environment" is a class—of perceptions, behaviors, actions and consequences—that does not include itself and therefore does not perceive its own limits. We could think that the human "world," being co-extensive with verbal language, is also a particularly developed environment: it would be the greatest possible *Umwelt*, that is, the class of all classes that do not include themselves. This is a suggestive but not particularly convincing hypothesis.[10] In effect, we should ask ourselves whether the class of all classes that do not include themselves includes itself or not. Either answer leads to an impasse: if it includes itself, the world-language is not an "environment"; if it does not include itself, it is not the class of *all* environments. The idea of the world-language as the *Umwelt* of all *Umwelten* is similar to the antinomy that, according to Russell, undermines Frege's work on the foundation of mathematics.

So, what is happening here? Between *Welt* and *Umwelt* there is a difference in nature, not in comprehensiveness. In fact, the two concepts exclude each other: if there is a world, there is no environment (or even better: there is a world because there is no environment). The sublime running against the limit and the aporias of self-reference show that the world-language is concerned with its own existence, that is, it is a function that takes itself as main argument. This is why man has no "environment" (if we indicate with this word a biological realm whose limits we do not perceive). On the other hand, we also see how language represents itself as unresolvable unknown, as "x" deprived of a determinate expression: this is the root of the Mystical. Having a world as *Welt* coincides fully with having a language, and is the source, for the Wittgenstein of the sublime, of the religious feeling. "My whole tendency [...] was to run against the boundaries of language. This running against the walls of our cage is perfectly, absolutely hopeless."[11]; nonetheless, Wittgenstein concludes that this tendency "means *something*."[12]

3. The *Investigations*, for an intransigent asceticism

The famous, or maybe infamous, issue of the continuity/discontinuity between the Wittgenstein of the *Tractatus* and the one of the *Investigations* should maybe be understood as the transition between the proud statement of the ascetic instance and its meticulous execution. Or more briefly: the grandiosity of the sublime is followed by the reserve of the mystical.

According to the truly ascetic Wittgenstein of the language games, the greatest error consists in wanting to show the ineffable obliquely, through the struggle against the limits of the sayable. Hence the polemics against the philosophical puzzles caused by the extravagant use of common words and the liquidation of the issues originating from the "vacancy" of language. In the *Philosophical Investigations* there are no boundaries to run against. Consequently, there is no way of indicating—not even in a purely negative manner through the self-immolation of representation—what really counts. Sublime procedures are now unthinkable. The sublime, in fact, is the propositional image of a worldly occurrence attempting to portray the existence of the world itself, thereby falling into an educational nonsense. In the *Investigations*, however, our language is no longer an image, but a gesture, a pragmatic component of a state of affairs; it is no longer a mirror, but the opaque ingredient of a form of life. If our propositions are not images of the world, but simple gestures, they cannot even fail or, by their failure, negatively and *e contrario* designate God. "So there must be perfect order even in the vaguest sentence."[13]

The logical form of the *Investigations* reminds us closely of the paradoxical dialectics between "penultimate" and "ultimate" things, as they are defined by the theologian Dietrich Bonhoeffer in his *Ethics*. The natural existence of human life is a "penultimate" thing: ways of life, language games, technologies, habits. Taken by itself, the penultimate-natural knows no lacks nor imperfections. It does not imply anything "ultimate" and therefore it doesn't suffer from its absence. The term "penultimate" can be deceiving, making us believe that the biological patrimony of the human animal is somehow in need of integration. This is not true at all: the "penultimate" is such only and precisely because it requires no improvement, and indeed it does not perceive itself as "penultimate." It is complete as it is, without doubts or premonitions. According to Bonhoeffer, a certain reality becomes penultimate "only from the point of view of the ultimate, that is, when it is devalued," and this occurs in spite of its natural perfection when there is a "justification of the sinner by grace only." In other words, "the penultimate is not a state or condition in itself, but it is a judgment which the ultimate passes upon that which has preceded it."[14] The ultimate reality is the free, autonomous word of God, which "implies the complete breaking off of everything that precedes it, of everything that is before the last; it is therefore never the natural or necessary end of the way which has been pursued so far, but it is rather the total condemnation and invalidation of this way, [...] it excludes any method of achieving it by a way of one's own."[15]

In the *Investigations*, there is no relation whatsoever between ultimate (God, what makes life worth living and so on) and penultimate things (the plurality of language games), not even a negative one. Therefore it would be wrong to keep talking about a caesura or a disproportion. The natural is not the opposite of the absolute; it does not lie at its borders, not even on the other side of an impassable threshold. If we take these theses to their extreme, the very concept of transcendence disappears. We no longer feel the absence of God in the world (like we did in the *Tractatus*). God is *not even* absent. Absolute immanence, and the retreat of all human practices in the realm of the penultimate finally delineates correctly the logical space of what lies beyond it. Only if we have no relation with it can the ultimate retain its status and appear as such. The opposite is also true: only if the propositions inherent to a certain language game contain no mysterious or defective quality—that is, nothing "penultimate"—will they reveal themselves, at a certain moment (when I think about my sins, for instance), as deprived of real importance, less valuable, "penultimate." Those who want to pray have to do so in secret, and most of all, thinking that God does not exist: this is the only true lesson of mystical asceticism.[16]

The following statement by Bonhoeffer could be a worthy epigraph to the *Investigations*: "Does one not in some cases, by remaining deliberately in the penultimate, perhaps point all the more genuinely to the ultimate, which God will speak in His own time (though indeed even with an human mouth)? Does not this mean that, over and over again, the penultimate will be what commends itself precisely for the sake of the ultimate, and that it will have to be done not with a heavy conscience but with a clear one?"[17] Wittgenstein doesn't seem to mean anything different when he writes:

> Where does our investigation gets its importance from, since it seems only to destroy everything interesting, that is, all that is great and important? (As it were all the buildings, leaving behind only bits of stone and rubble.) What we are destroying is nothing but houses of cards and we are clearing up the ground of language on which they stand.[18]

What looks great and important is the *non-comprehended* that metaphysics keeps fussing about; this has to be eliminated through a naturalistic reconstruction of the behaviors of the human animal. But this elimination has to occur for one main reason: because it usurps the place reserved to what is really *incomprehensible*.

"Penultimate things," then, are self-sufficient and deprived of mystery. In their case, one can no longer use the emphatic concept of boundary. We need to reread the paragraph 499 of the *Investigations* in its totality:

> To say "This combination of words makes no sense" excludes it from the sphere of language and thereby bounds the domain of

> language. But when one draws a boundary it may be for various kinds of reason. If I surround an area with a fence or a line or otherwise, the purpose may be to prevent someone from getting in or out; but it may also be a part of a game and the players be supposed, say, to jump over the boundary; or it may shew where the property of one man ends and that of another begins; and so on. So if I draw a boundary line that is not yet to say what I am drawing it for.[19]

The evaporation of the boundary inevitably falls back on the issue of self-reference. Instead of staging yet another sublime failure, the latter becomes trivial. It suffices to think about the following passage from the *Investigations*:

> When I talk about language (words, sentences, etc.) I must speak the language of every day. Is this language somehow too coarse and material for what we want to say? Then how is another one to be constructed?—And how strange that we should be able to do anything at all with the one we have! In giving explanations I already have to use language full-blown (not some sort of preparatory, provisional one): this by itself shews that I can adduce only exterior facts about language. Yes, but then how can these explanations satisfy us?—Well, your very questions were framed in this language; they had to be expressed in this language, if there was anything to ask! And your scruples are misunderstandings. Your questions refer to words; so I have to talk about words.[20]

The vicious circles of linguistic self-referentiality are neutralized and even mocked. Since there are no unitary and inescapable boundaries to overstep, I can speak about language with the same perspicuous imprecision that I speak about a lamp or a table. All falls within the realm of the "penultimate": all speech about speech is only another possible speech. All affirmations about the world as totality are only a fact of the world. But this is precisely the point: the realm of the "penultimate"—without gaps nor fissures—assumes the appearance of an *Umwelt*, of an environment whose boundaries we cannot perceive. Since language is no longer a function that can talk—however aporetically—of its own existence, the "world" seems to share the defining traits of an "environment." The passage from the *Tractatus* to the *Investigations*, from sublime chatter to impeccable asceticism, also implies the seemingly paradoxical transformation of the *Welt* into a kind of fictitious *Umwelt*.

If the coextensive relation between world and language that distinguishes the *Tractatus* reproduces the one between Father and Son, in the *Investigations* we see the contours of the Holy Ghost: the natural community of speakers. A community that, abandoning all transcendent pride, configures a biological-mystical *Umwelt* where we always have to stick to penultimate realities, and to do it in good conscience precisely for the sake of the ultimate. In the journals of 1936–1937, which were written at the same time of the *Investigations*, Wittgenstein fixed thus the true statute of the biological-mystical *Umwelt*: "But let us talk in our mother tongue, and not believe that that we have to pull ourselves out of the swamp by our own hair [...]. We are only supposed to remove the misunderstandings, after all. I think this is a good sentence. To God alone be praise!"[21]

4. For an atheistic critique of Wittgenstein

It would certainly be possible to spend a few words defending metaphysics against its religious critique. When Wittgenstein says that philosophical problems arise from a vacancy of language, he is clearly right. However, one can reply that such a "vacancy," that is, the baroque use of certain words outside of common language games, is a way (by the way, a very *natural* one) to express the essential questions of our existence, the fact of being so-and-so. "A *misunderstanding* makes it look to us as if a proposition *did* something queer."[22] No, we could answer, it is us who, sometimes, thinking about the meaning of life, do something queer with our propositions. Just as we do something queer, by the way, when we build a formalized language adequate to scientific knowledge. Talking about the word this, for instance, Wittgenstein adds that "a queer use of this word [...] doubtlessly only occurs in doing philosophy."[23] This is certainly so, but what matters most is which real problem is alluded to by using "this" in a strange way, and also what kind of philosophy can support one of the different strange uses of the demonstrative pronoun (the Aristotelian *tode ti*, the Hegelian *Diese*, or Russell's *This*). And so on. It seems evident, though, that this kind of argumentation would appear weak and useless, not much better than legalistic jabber.

The real issue is trying to build an atheistic critique of metaphysics. This is the only interesting countermove to be played against Wittgenstein. The issue of atheism, no matter how outdated and discredited, becomes once more a quintessentially theoretical—that is, logical-linguistic—theme. Far from being a petty inquiry into private inclinations and idiosyncrasies, an analysis of Wittgenstein's positions shows how far empiricist naturalism and religious instance can proceed together, in a complementary and functional manner, instead of canceling each other out. This is why it would be incongruous to oppose naturalist reasons to the mystical critique of metaphysics. Thus, an atheist (not simply materialist) metacritique is in order. We can't do it here, of course. What we can do, however, is to sketch its contours, as we do for a still unattended task.

What really matters is to describe differently the conceptual constellation constituted by three keywords: boundary, self-reference and world. Wittgenstein's religious demolition of philosophy is built upon these concepts. Therefore, any attempt at creating a logical-linguistic atheism has to deal with them too. Let us sum things up. In the *Tractatus*, self-reference resolves itself by running against the boundaries of our visual field: this is a sublime clash alluding to what transcends both our world and our language. In the *Investigations*, self-reference is neutralized: there is no boundary to be discerned within the "penultimate" (which can be compared to a pseudo-*Umwelt*), everything is just right as it is. In the first case, self-reference is impossible, in the second one it is trivial. If this is how things stand, then an atheist metacritique has to operate a double cross-step.

First of all, we need to reinstate the difference (a difference in nature, and not in degree) between *Welt* and *Umwelt*, "world" and "environment," which in the last Wittgenstein becomes less and less defined and ends up almost disappearing. The multiplicity of life forms and language games does not contradict, but actually makes more real and pertinent, the definition of the world as the function that takes itself as object of study, that is, a field problematizing its own boundaries. The fact that single systems of life habits (with their specific grammars) are not organized as a hierarchy of logical classes, and can only be enumerated through the conjunctions and disjunctions of propositional calculus, does not prevent them from exhibiting, *each* in its unique way, a *common* boundary. We could therefore say that we go from the *Investigations* to the *Tractatus*, at least for the inextricable bond between *Welt* and *Grenze*, world and boundaries.

This is where we enter the second, decisive stage of an atheistic metacritique. I will start its elucidation with a series of rhetorical questions. Is it really true that the limits of my language are the limits of my world? Shouldn't we question this coincidence? When Wittgenstein talks about going beyond the world, *that is*, beyond signifying language, is this "*that is*" really justified? Shouldn't we rather posit a fundamental asymmetry between these two terms and, therefore, their partial and reciprocal excess? These questions help us define a line of argumentation that can be illustrated by three basic assertions: 1. Rather than corresponding to each other and sharing the same boundaries, language and world intersect like the x- and y- axes and then continue on independently. 2. The material-sensory world transcends our language because it is the exorbitant context of our speech. 3. Language, however, also transcends the world that exceeds and includes it: the world, in fact, only becomes the inescapable context of every experience only because it is inhabited by speech (that is, literally, by a text). 4. The sensible world as "beyond" of language is still something that can be *perceived*; similarly, language as "beyond" of the sensible world is still something that can be *enunciated*. In both cases we are not dealing with a true "beyond" (that would be neither worldly nor linguistic). 5. The mutual transcendence of sensorial perception and articulate speech excludes a properly theological transcendence. 6. An atheistic critique of metaphysics (and of Wittgenstein) maybe is summed up in a simple observation; the limits of my language *are not* the limits of my world.

Notes

Preface

1. See P. Virno, *A Grammar of the Multitude* (Los Angeles: Semiotext(e), 2004), 7–19.

2. Ibid., 13.

Introduction

1. [Available in French and German; this book has not been translated into English.]

2. [Virno refers to the protests against the 2001 G20 meeting in Genoa, where the object of contestation was the current—cognitive and linguistic—incarnation of capitalist command. The protests incurred the exceptionally violent reaction of the Italian police, which killed one activist and wounded many others.]

1. The Speaker as Performing Artist

1. F. de Saussure, *Course in General Linguistics* (New York: Philosophical Library, 1959), 18.

2. Aristotle, *The Nicomachean Ethics of Aristotle*, trans. F. H. Peters (London: Kegan Paul, Trench & Co., 1886), 186.

3. Ibid., 187

4. H. Arendt, "What is Freedom," in *Between Past and Future: Eight Exercises in Political Thought* (New York: Penguin Books, 1977), 154.

5. E. Benveniste, "Subjectivity in Language," in *Problems in General Linguistics* (Coral Gables, FL: University of Miami Press, 1971), 223–224.

6. L. Wittgenstein, *Philosophical Investigations*, trans. G. E. M. Anscombe (Cambridge: Blackwell, 1997), 130–131e.

7. Wittgenstein, *Philosophical Grammar*, ed. Rush Rhees, trans. Anthony Kenny (Oxford: Blackwell, 1974), 19.

8. Ibid., 184–5.

9. Wittgenstein, *Philosophical Investigations*, 138e.

10. Wittgenstein, *Philosophical Grammar*, 184.

11. Benveniste, "The Nature of the Linguistic Sign," in op. cit., 48.

12. Wittgenstein, op. cit., 184.

13. Ibid., 192.

14. For a discussion of this theme, see D. W. Winnicott, *Playing and Reality* (London: Tavistock/Routledge, 1971), 100 and following.

15. Ibid., 79.

16. Ibid., 62.

17. Ibid., 49.

18. Saussure, op. cit., 119–120.

19. Aristotle, *Metaphysics Theta*, trans. S. Makin (Oxford: Clarendon Press, 2006), 11.

20. Benveniste, "The Formal Apparatus of the Enunciation," in *The Discourse Studies Reader: Main Currents in Theory and Analysis*, eds. J. Angermuller, D. Mainguenau, and R. Wodak (Amsterdam/Philadelphia: John Benjamins Publishing Company, 2014), 141.

21. Ibid., 142.

22. Ibid., 143.

23. Benveniste, "The Nature of Pronouns," in *Problems in General Linguistics*, 218.

24. Benveniste, "The Formal Apparatus of the Enunciation," 143.

25. Arendt, "The *Vita Activa* and the Modern Age," in *The Human Condition* (Chicago: University of Chicago Press, 1958), 289–296.

26. Gottlob Frege, "On Sense and Meaning," in *Collected Papers on Mathematics, Logic, and Philosophy* (Oxford/New York: Blackwell, 1984), 163.

27. E. Husserl, *Logical Investigations*, vol. 1 (London/New York: Routledge 2001), 189.

28. [General Charles De Gaulle said these words during WW1, when asked how the "intendance," the personnel charged with the logistics of a military operation, would deal with the practicalities of his daring battle plan. He answered that "the personnel would follow," underscoring that when the plan is clear, all other details will fall into place. This expression is now proverbial in French and other linguistic contexts.]

2. The Absolute Performative

1. See Saussure, op. cit., 9.

2. Wittgenstein, *Tractatus Logico-Philosophicus* (Mineola, NY: Dover, 1999), 107.

3. B. Malinowski, "The Problem of Meaning in Primitive Languages," in *The Meaning of Meaning*, eds. C. K. Ogden and I. A. Richards (New York: Harcourt, 1923), 296–335, 315.

4. Ibid.

5. J. L. Austin, *How To Do Things With Words* (Boston: Harvard University Press, 1962), 6.

6. Ibid., 64.

7. Ibid.

8. See Benveniste, "Delocutive Verbs," in op. cit., 240–242.

9. Ibid., 245.

10. Wittgenstein, *Philosophical Investigations*, 132e.

11. Frege, "Thoughts," in op. cit., 358 and following.

12. Austin, op. cit., 14.

13. Ibid., 19.

14. Ibid., 21.

15. J. Piaget, *The Language and Thought of the Child* (New York: Routledge, 1952), 12.

16. Ibid., 14.

17. Ibid., 15 and following.

18. L. Vygotsky, *Thought and Word* (Boston: Harvard University Press), 136.

19. Ibid., 133.

20. See F. Cimatti, *La scimmia che si parla. Linguaggio autocoscienza e libertà nell'animale umano* (Torino: Bollati Boringhieri, 2000).

21. Husserl, *Logical Investigations*, vol. 1 (London/New York: Routledge, 2001), 190 and following.

22. Ibid., 191.

23. Ibid.

24. E. de Martino, *La fine del mondo. Contributo all'analisi delle apocalissi culturali* (Torino: Einaudi, 2002), 231.

25. Benveniste, "La blasphémie et l'euphémie," in *Problèmes de linguistique générale*, vol. 2 (Paris: Gallimard, 1974), 254–257, 255. [The essay is not available in English; the translation is mine.—Trans.]

26. Ibid.

27. G. Van der Leeuw, *Religion in Essence and Manifestation* (Princeton: Princeton University Press, 1986), 420.

28. Ibid., 409.

29. Ibid.

30. Benveniste, "Delocutive Verbs," 245.

31. Van Der Leeuw, op. cit., 405–406.

32. Ibid., 432.

33. C. Herrenschmidt, "Writing Between Visible and Invisible Worlds in Iran, Israel and Greece," in *Ancestor of the West. Writing, Reasoning and Religion in Mesopotamia, Elam and Greece*, eds. J. Bottéro, C. Herrenschmidt, and J. Vernant (Chicago/London: University of Chicago Press, 2000), 110.

34. Van der Leeuw, op. cit., 432.

35. P. Florensky, *Il valore magico della parola* (Milano: Medusa, 2001), 76. [The original Russian essay, "Mysl' i Jazyk," is not available in English translation. I translate from the Italian edition.—Trans.]

36. Van der Leeuw, op. cit., 420.

37. Ibid., 421.

38. L. Feuerbach, *The Essence of Christianity* (New York: Cosimo Books, 2008), 153.

39. Augustine, "The Teacher," in *Against the Academicians and The Teacher* (Indianapolis: Hackett Publishing, 1995), 94–146, 95.

40. Ibid., 96.

41. Ibid., 118.

42. E. Minkowski, *Lived Time: Phenomenological and Psychopathological Studies* (Chicago: Northwestern University Press, 1970), 106.

43. P. Tillich, *The Courage To Be* (New Haven/London: Yale University Press, 2000), 187.

44. S. Weil, *Gravity and Grace* (London/New York: Routledge, 2002), 27.

45. Ibid., 34.

3. The Repetition of Anthropogenesis

1. De Martino, *Primitive Magic. The Psychic Powers of Shamans and Sorcerers* (Lindfield: Bay Books, 1972), 146–147.

2. De Martino, *La fine del mondo*, 85.

3. Ibid., 74.

4. Saussure, op. cit., 9.

5. Benveniste, "The Formal Apparatus," 142.

6. Benveniste, "Animal Communication and Human Language," in *Problems in General Linguistics*, 49–54, 54.

7. Ibid., 49–54, 53.

8. Benveniste, "The Formal Apparatus," 143.

9. See Virno, *Il ricordo del presente. Saggio sul tempo storico* (Torino: Bollati Boringhieri, 1999).

10. De Martino, op. cit., 89.

11. Ibid.

12. Ibid., 90.

13. Ibid., 670.

14. Ibid., 174.

15. De Martino, *Storia e metastoria. I fondamenti di una teoria del sacro* (Lecce: Argo Editore, 1995), 173.

4. Second-degree Sensualism: A Physiognomic Project

1. Part of this chapter is a modified version of my contribution to an essay written with Marco Mazzeo, "Il fisiologico come simbolo del logico. Wittgenstein fisionomo," in *Sensibilita' e linguaggio. Un seminario su Wittgenstein*, eds. M. De Carolis and A. Martone (Macerata: Quodlibet, 2002).

2. See T. W. Deacon, *The Symbolic Species: The Co-evolution of Language and the Brain* (New York: Norton, 1997), 309 and following.

3. [In Italian, the word is *aiuola*, whose pronunciation is based on the liquid consonant "l" and three vowels.]

4. Wittgenstein, op. cit., 209e.

5. Ibid.

6. Ibid.

7. Ibid., 197e.

8. Aristotle, *Metaphysics*, trans. W. D. Ross (Oxford: Oxford University Press, 1908), http://classics.mit.edu/Aristotle/metaphysics.9.ix.html.

9. Wittgenstein, op. cit., 199e.

10. Wittgenstein, op. cit., 208e.

11. Ibid., 200e.

12. Ibid.

13. Wittgenstein, *The Brown Book*, in *The Blue and Brown Books* (Oxford: Blackwell, 1958), 135–136.

14. Wittgenstein, *Philosophical Investigations*, 216e.

15. Wittgenstein, "Lecture on Ethics," *The Philosophical Review* 74, no. 1 (Jan. 1965): 3–12, 8.

16. Wittgenstein, *Philosophical investigations*, 193e.

17. Frege, *The Foundations of Arithmetic* (Evanston: Northwestern University Press, 1980), 64–65.

18. Ibid., 65.

19. Wittgenstein, op. cit., 212e.

20. Ibid., 196e.

21. [In English in the original.]

22. Wittgenstein, op. cit., 228e.

23. E. Gombrich, *Art and Illusion. A Study in the Psychology of Pictorial Representation* (New York: Pantheon Books, 1960), 330.

24. Wittgenstein, *Tractatus Logico-Philosophicus*, 40.

25. Ibid., 40.

26. Wittgensein, *Philosophical Investigations*, 193e.

27. Ibid., 197e.

28. Ibid., 210e.

29. Wittgenstein, *The Brown Book*, 165.

30. Ibid., 165.

31. Ibid., 165.

32. Ibid., 166.

33. Ibid.

34. Ibid., 167.

35. ["To rust." In the Italian original the double "r" and double "g" force the speaker to slow down the enunciation.]

36. Wittgenstein, *Philosophical Investigations*, 218e.

37. F. Lo Piparo, "Le signe linguistique est-il à deux faces?," *Cahiers Ferdinand de Saussure* 45 (1991): 213–221, 219.

38. Wittgenstein, op. cit., 223e.

39. Ibid., 228e.

5. In Praise of Reification

1. B. Russell, "Knowledge by Acquaintance and Knowledge by Description," in *Mysticism and Logic* (New York: Doubleday, 1957), 205–206.

2. K. Marx, *Capital*, vol. 1 (London: Electric Book Company, 2002), 104–105.

3. Ibid., 120.

4. Winnicott, *Human Nature* (London: Free Association Books, 1988), 106–111.

5. G. Simondon, *Du mode d'existence des objets techniques* (Paris: Aubier, 1958), 248. [The book is not available in English. The translation is mine.—Trans.]

6. Ibid., 245.

7. Ibid., 241.

8. See Marx, *Grundrisse*, trans. D. McLellan (New York: Harper and Row), 141–143.

9. Piparo, op. cit., 213–221, 218.

10. Benveniste, "Categories of Thought and Language," in *Problems in General Linguistics*, 55–64.

11. I. Kant, *Critique of Pure Reason* (New York: Penguin Classics, 2007), 319.

12. Ibid., 326.

13. Ibid., 324.

14. S. Freud, "The Uncanny," in *The Standard Edition of the Complete Psychological Works of Sigmund Freud*, vol. 17, trans. J. Strachey (London: Hogarth Press, 1955), http://web.mit.edu/allanmc/www/freud1.pdf, 9.

15. G. W. F. Hegel, *Introductory Lectures on Aesthetics*, trans. B. Bosanquet (London: Penguin, 1993), 70

16. Ibid., 72

17. Ibid.

18. Kant, op. cit., A355.

19. Ibid.

20. Ibid., A356.

21. Ibid., A363.

22. [In the Italian original, Virno uses the name of the soccer club *Roma*.]

23. Kant, op. cit., 238, B275.

24. Ibid., 239, B276.

25. [The French title of Ponge's famous collection is *Le Parti pris des choses*, which I translate here "an allegiance to things," although in English it often appears as *The Voice of Things*.]

26. See the end of F. Shelling, *Philosophie der Offenbarung* (Berlin: Surhkamp Verlag, 1993). [Not available in English translation.—Trans.]

6. Natural History

1. See W. Benjamin, *The Origin of German Tragic Drama* (London: Verso, 1994), 167 and following.

2. T. Adorno, "The Idea of Natural History," *TELOS* 60 (June 20, 1984): 111–124, 117.

3. N. Chomsky and M. Foucault, *On Human Nature* (New York: The New Press, 2006), 7.

4. Ibid.

5. Ibid., 26–27.

6. Ibid., 33.

7. Ibid., 37–38.

8. Ibid., 58.

9. Ibid., 50.

10. Ibid., 29–30.

11. Feuerbach, op. cit., 152 and following.

12. S. Timpanaro, *Sul materialismo* (Pisa: Nistri-Lischi, 1975), 48.

13. De Martino, *La fine del mondo*, 378.

14. Ibid., 390.

15. D. Marconi, *Filosofia e scienza cognitiva* (Roma: Laterza, 2001), 127 and following.

16. Ibid., 127.

17. Saussure, op. cit., 160.

18. Ibid., 18.

19. Virno, *Il ricordo del presente. Saggio sul tempo storico* (Torino: Bollati Boringhieri 1999), 69–71.

20. Saussure, op. cit., 9.

21. Piparo, "Due paradigmi linguistici a confronto," in *Le vie di Babele. Percorsi di storiografia linguistica* (1600–1800), eds. D. Di Cesare and S. Gensini (Casale Monferrato: Marietti, 1987), 1–9, 6.

22. A. Leroi-Gourhan, *Gesture and Speech* (Cambridge/London: MIT Press, 1993), 117–118.

23. J. G. Herder, "Treatise on the Origin of Language," in *Philosophical Writings*, trans. and ed. M. N. Forster (New York: Cambridge University Press, 2002), 65–162, 77–78.

24. Ibid., 80.

25. E. H. Lennerberg, *Biological Foundations of Language* (New York: John Wiley and Sons, 1967), 174.

26. K. Lorenz, *Motivation of Human and Animal Behavior: An Ethological View* (New York: Van Rostrand Reinhold, 1973), 83–84.

27. See Virno, op. cit., 67 and following.

28. Chomsky , *Language and Problems of Knowledge: The Managua Lectures* (Boston: MIT Press, 1987), p. 151,

29. See Virno, op. cit., 71, 92 and following.

30. De Martino, op. cit., 9.

31. Ibid., 632.

32. Ibid., 91.

33. Marx, *The Economic and Philosophic Manuscripts of 1844* (New York: International Publishers, 1964), 142.

34. Ibid., 143.

35. C. W. Peirce, *Collected Papers 1931–58*, vol. 3 (Cambridge: Harvard University Press, 1933), 211.

36. Ibid. vol. 4, 414.

37. Wittgenstein, *Tractatus Logico-Philosophicus*, 53.

7. The Multitude and the Principle of Individuation

1. This chapter was already published in Italian as the postface to the Italian edition of a classic book by Georges Simondon, *L'individuazione psichica e collettiva* (Roma: DeriveApprodi, 2001).

2. T. Hobbes, *De Cive or The Citizen* (New York: Appleton-Century-Croft, 1982), 135.

3. See Virno, *Mondanità. L'idea di "mondo" tra esperienza sensibile e sfera pubblica*, Roma: DeriveApprodi 1994 and *A Grammar of the Multitude*, New York: Semiotext(e) 2004.

4. Simondon, *L'individuation psychique et collective* (Paris: Aubier, 2007), 196. [Simondon's book has not been translated into English. All translations from the original French are mine.—Trans.]

5. M. Merleau-Ponty, *Phenomenology of Perception* (New York: Humanities Press, 1962), 215.

6. Ibid., 347.

7. Simondon, op. cit., 210.

8. Ibid., 204.

9. Ibid., 111.

10. Ibid., 193.

11. Ibid., 205.

Appendix: Wittgenstein and the Question of Atheism

1. Besides wondering at the existence of the world, Wittgenstein mentions a second miraculous, and therefore ethical, feeling, the experience of feeling absolutely safe. If wondering pertains mostly to our ability to know, inhabiting its limits, safety mostly pertains to our practical destiny. These two different forms of miracle fully coincide with the Kantian separation of the sublime in two fundamental species: the mathematical and the dynamic. The mathematical sublime is the emotion provoked by the *greatness* of the world: considered in its totality, nature is infinitely big, incommensurable with the extension and duration of sensory phenomena. The dynamic sublime, instead, is caused by the frightening *power* of the world and the consideration of what could constitute an absolute protection against such danger. (See Virno, *Mondanità. L'idea di "mondo" tra esperienza sensibile e sfera pubblica* [Roma: Manifestolibri ,1994], 11–33.)

2. Wittgenstein, op. cit, 107.

3. Ibid., 107.

4. Wittgenstein, "A Lecture on Ethics," *The Philosophical Review* 74, no. 1 (Jan., 1965): 3–12, 11.

5. Wittgenstein, *Tractatus Logico-Philosophicus*, 53.

6. Wittgenstein, "A Lecture on Ethics," 11.

7. F. Waismann, *Wittgenstein and the Vienna Circle* (Lanham: Rowman and Littlefield, 1979), 107 and following.

8. Wittgenstein, *Tractatus Logico-Philosophicus*, 88.

9. Wittgenstein, "A Lecture on Ethics," 11.

10. Franco Lo Piparo, in his essay "Il mondo, le specie animali e il linguaggio. La teoria zoocognitiva del Tractatus," published in *Percezione linguaggio coscienza. Saggi di filosofia della mente*, eds. M. Carenini and M. Matteuzzi (Macerata: Quodlibet, 1999), has proposed a similarity between the linguistic world described in the Tractatus and the zoological concept of *Umwelt*. In our argument we develop an implicit objection to this thesis.

11. Wittgenstein, op. cit., 11–12.

12. Ibid., 13.

13. Wittgenstein, *Philosophical Investigations*, 45e.

14. D. Bonhoeffer, *Ethics* (New York: McMillan, 1955), 133.

15. Ibid., 123.

16. In the journals of 1936–1937, Wittgenstein writes: "After a day difficult for me, I kneeled during dinner today and prayed and suddenly said, kneeling and looking up above: 'There is no one here.' That made me feel at ease [...] But that does not mean, for example: I had previously been in error." *Wittgenstein, Wittgenstein: Public and Private Occasions* (Lanham, MD: Rowman and Littlefield, 2010), 202.

17. Ibid., 126.

18. Wittgenstein, *Philosophical Investigations*, 207e.

19. Ibid., 139e.

20. Ibid., 50e. Here, Wittgenstein also writes: "One might think: if philosophy speaks of the use of the word 'philosophy' there must be a second-order philosophy. But it is not so: it is, rather, like the case of orthography, which deals with the word 'orthography' among others without then being second-order."

21. Wittgenstein, *Public and Private Occasions*, 243.

22. Wittgenstein, *Philosophical Investigations*, 44e.

23. Ibid., 19e.